S0-BZP-663

Ernie

STEPHEN McGEE

THE ROSTER

EDITOR
Kevin Bull

DESIGNER
Ryan Ford

PHOTO EDITOR
Diane Weiss

PROJECT COORDINATOR
Steve Dorsey

COPY EDITORS
Mari delaGarza,
Tim Marcinkoski

PHOTO TONING
Charles Whitman
Ken Elenich
Erin Fuhs

COVER PHOTO
Mandi Wright

COVER DESIGN
Steve Dorsey

SPORTS EDITOR
Gene Myers

SPECIAL THANKS
Patricia Anstett,
Jo-Ann Barnas,
Laurie Delves,
Tom Panzenhagen,
Ric Simon,
S. Gary Spicer Sr.,
Mike Thompson,
Shawn Windsor,
Mandi Wright and the
Anchor Bar

OTHER FREE PRESS TIGERS BOOKS

- The Corner
- Roar Restored
- Not Till the Fat Lady Sings
- Century of Champions
- Corner to CoPa

To order any of these titles or other gear, go to freep.com/bookstore or call 800-245-5082.

> WELL, DON'T JUST STAND THERE LIKE THE HOUSE BY THE SIDE OF THE ROAD!

ERNIE HARWELL
1918-2010

MIKE THOMPSON

OTHER BOOKS FROM THE VOICE OF SUMMER

Ernie Harwell, the acclaimed voice of the Detroit Tigers, had one of the longest runs by a broadcaster with one major league club, calling Tigers games for 42 seasons. For the first 32 of those seasons, he made and cemented his legacy by doing play-by-play on the radio. His Southern voice — rich and authoritative but not overbearing — became as distinctive to Michigan listeners as baseball itself. But in addition to his years on the air, he's also an author, penning four books for the Free Press:

 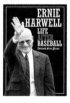 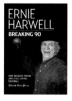 

STORIES FROM MY LIFE IN BASEBALL
The beloved Tigers broadcaster tells wonderful stories from his life in baseball. It's the first of four collections of his Free Press columns.

LIFE AFTER BASEBALL
Though he was retired from the booth, Ernie Harwell was active as ever. This collection of columns will help you recall those days when the transistor radio lived under your pillow.

BREAKING 90
As he approached his 90th birthday in January 2008, Hall of Fame broadcaster Ernie Harwell shared nine decades of baseball wit and wisdom in this third collection of his Free Press columns.

EXTRA INNINGS WITH THE VOICE OF SUMMER
In his fourth book in a series based on his Free Press columns, Ernie Harwell shared more timeless baseball stories and answered readers' questions.

Detroit Free Press

615 W. Lafayette Blvd.
Detroit, MI 48226
©2010 by Detroit Free Press. All rights reserved.

 TRIUMPH

Published by Triumph Books

No part of this book may be reproduced or transmitted in any form or by any means, electronic or mechanical, including photocopying, recording or by an information storage system, without the permission of the publisher, except where permitted by law.

TABLE OF CONTENTS

KIRTHMON F. DOZIER

THE GOOD LIFE

CALLS FROM THE VOICE OF SUMMER

APRIL 11, 2000: *THE FIRST GAME AT COMERICA PARK, A 5-2 VICTORY OVER SEATTLE:*

"WELL, HERE WE GO. MCLEMORE WILL LEAD IT OFF. HERE'S THE FIRST PITCH AT COMERICA — AND IT'S A STRIKE CALLED. I TALKED TO MAC BEFORE THE GAME. I SAID, 'EVER DONE ANYTHING LIKE THAT BEFORE?' HE SAID, 'NO, BUT I'M READY.' "

He was ready, but we weren't

BY MITCH ALBOM

The Voice of Summer died in the spring, just before the Tigers' first pitch of the evening. That was fitting. Ernie Harwell never wanted to interrupt the game. Mr. "Looong Gone" is gone now. Like the home run that lands in the seats, like the final out of the ninth inning, like the thousands of games he closed with his signature sign-offs, his genteel voice telling us he'd see us tomorrow. At 92, after a battle with bile duct cancer that stretched into extra innings, Ernie let go of this world and moved on to the higher place from which we were certain he was sent.

Gone now. We knew this was coming. Ernie, in his final grace, prepared us for it. He told us not to worry. We still worried. He told us not to cry. We cried anyhow. He told us he had led the life he'd wanted, that he was ready to say good-bye.

But we were not.

"I know into whose arms I'm gonna fall," he told me in one of our last conversations, on a brightly lit stage in front of a sold-out Fox Theatre, a last, packed-house tribute to a man who became arguably the most popular figure in the history of our state simply by doing the same gentle thing over and over, calling baseball games, remaining

CONTINUED ON PAGE 8

ROMAIN BLANQUART

A MAN LOVED BY ALL

Detroit has seen Hall of Fame athletes in every sport and colorful superstars and brilliant coaches and some excellent sportscasters. But there has never been anybody like Ernie Harwell. He even thanked media members before his farewell speech at Comerica Park on Sept. 16, 2009.

 Ernie

HEAVENLY FIGURE

In one of his last conversations with Mitch Albom, on a wide stage in front of a sold-out Fox Theatre in Detroit on Sept. 30, 2009, Ernie said what his cancer taught him: "I can really know where I'm going, and what a great, great thing heaven is going to be."

CONTINUED FROM PAGE 6

consistent, pure, good and true, even as the world around him became anything but. Ernie stood out because he stood still. He was reliable as a rock. A soul in a void. A heart in an often heartless time.

As long as there was Ernie, there was still a piece of childhood, of summers gone by, of what baseball was supposed to be about, a pastime, a joyous diversion, youth — good, sweet, innocent youth. Even after Harwell stopped broadcasting nearly eight years ago, just knowing he was here, seeing him on occasion at the stadium, his hands dug in his back pockets, that wide grin beneath a funny beret, made us feel that things were still OK in baseball, because the Voice of Summer was still around, watching over the game.

Gone now.

Normally, when a sports hero dies, those of us on the inside can share the unique perspective of "a person who knew him." But everybody knew Ernie. If you heard him, you knew him. If you met him, you knew him. He was that rare thing, a man the same on the front side and the back.

Maybe I can tell you a few things. The way he re-enacted games in his early days as a voice of the Atlanta Crackers, following the action on ticker-tape, then broadcasting with sound effects, as if it happened in front of him. Sometimes, he once told me, if the machine broke down, he'd have to invent a reason for the delay.

"Uh-oh, a dog just ran on the field," he'd say, or something like that. Ernie laughed at those memories. But isn't imagination the key to baseball on the radio? Didn't you paint pictures to Ernie's words as

KATHLEEN GALLIGAN

he called the action — "the crafty left-hander" on the mound, or the batter who "stood there like the house by the side of the road"?

Over time, Ernie's voice became the soundtrack of our internal movies, until the game became a story — narrated by the most alluring storyteller. I once said if baseball could talk, it would sound like Ernie Harwell — unhurried, slightly southern, as comfortable as an old couch.

Ernie wrote that his heroes were sports writers. I guess this business loved him for that. But I can tell you that whenever a new sports writer or broadcaster came to town, Ernie would greet him as if welcoming an immigrant relative off the ship. Never once did he swing his weight. Never did he let his years of service drape him in an air of superiori-

CONTINUED ON PAGE 11

MEET ERNIE

HIS LIFE
FULL NAME: William Earnest Harwell.
BORN: Jan. 25, 1918, in Washington, Ga.
DIED: May 4, 2010, in Novi, Mich.

FAMILY
PARENTS: Gray and Helen Harwell.
BROTHERS: Davis and Dick Harwell.
WIFE: Lulu Harwell. They were married for 68 years.
CHILDREN: William Harwell, Gray Harwell, Julie Harwell and Carolyn Raley. Seven grandchildren and seven great-grandchildren.

EDUCATION
Emory University (1940). He later received honorary degrees from the University of Michigan, Wayne State University, Northern Michigan University and Adrian College.

EARLY OCCUPATIONS
Atlanta correspondent for the Sporting News (1934-48), sports writer for the Atlanta Constitution (1936-40), sports director for WSB radio in Atlanta (1940-42).

BASEBALL BROADCASTING CAREER
Atlanta Crackers (1943, 1946-48), Brooklyn Dodgers (1948-49), N.Y. Giants (1950-53), Baltimore Orioles (1954-59), Detroit Tigers (1960-91, 1993-2002).

AWARDS
Ford C. Frick Award from Baseball Hall of Fame (1981), National Sportscasters and Sportswriters Association Hall of Fame (1989), Michigan Sports Hall of Fame (1989), Radio Hall of Fame (1998), Vin Scully Lifetime Achievement Award in Sports Broadcasting (2010).

BY THE NUMBERS
8,500: Approximate television and radio broadcasts between 1948 and 2002.
6,687: Approximate Tigers' broadcasts.
2: Games missed in his 55-year major league career (his brother's funeral in 1968 and his induction into National Sportscasters and Sportswriters Association Hall of Fame in 1989).

ERNIE HARWELL WOULD SAY THIS "VOICE OF THE TURTLE" PASSAGE FROM SONG OF SOLOMON BEFORE THE EXHIBITION OPENER EACH YEAR DURING SPRING TRAINING:

"FOR, LO, THE WINTER IS PAST,

THE RAIN IS OVER AND GONE;

THE FLOWERS APPEAR ON THE EARTH;

THE TIME OF THE SINGING OF BIRDS IS COME,

AND THE VOICE OF THE TURTLE IS HEARD IN OUR LAND."

NEVER SKIPPING A BEAT

Ernie jumps rope in his Farmington Hills home at age 85. Known for his daily fitness routine, he helped head up a statewide effort by Blue Cross Blue Shield to get Michigan residents walking. He served as Blue Cross Blue Shield health and fitness advocate since 2004.

HUGH GRANNUM

10

CONTINUED FROM PAGE 9

ty. He made humility his calling card. He shook hands with new pitchers or center-fielders and drawled, "Welcome to the Tigahs" or "Good to have ya here," and it would be someone else who would nudge the new guy and say, "Do you know who that was? That was Ernie Harwell. THE Ernie Harwell."

No one ever earned a "THE" more than him.

An outsider may wonder why so many fans today are singing Ernie's praises, but it was largely because he never sang his own. In a sport full of big egos, Ernie's was invisible.

Gone now. Ernie died quietly, at home, with his wife and children by his side, and when the news was announced in Minnesota, where the Tigers were playing, fans there gave him a standing ovation. In Minnesota!

But then, Harwell was so much more than an announcer. He was a voice inside of us as well as outside of us. A voice you still can hear, even though the world has silenced it. He was a man to admire, a satisfied soul, a shining example of life lived purely and honestly. And because of that, Ernie will live on inside everyone who ever met him, shook his hand, gave him a hug, or simply heard his soothing words come through a tiny speaker in a car radio, or through an earphone hidden from the teacher on a school day afternoon.

In his last appearance at the stadium last year, he told the crowd, "The blessed part of (my) journey is that it's going to end here in the great state of Michigan."

And one last time, his call was on the money. Ernie Harwell, the Voice of Summer, is now, as they say in the game he loved, in the books. But his page will be read again and again, and remembered lovingly by any of us lucky to have heard, met or known him. Gone now. But not forgotten. Never forgotten. You don't forget.

COURTESY OF THE DAN DICKERSON COLLECTION

MADE FOR THE MICROPHONE

Ernie, seated, got his start with the Atlanta Crackers of the Southern League. Shown here in 1947, he worked with the Crackers until 1948 when he was traded to the Brooklyn Dodgers for catcher Cliff Dapper.

COURTESY OF THE GARY SPICER COLLECTION

MEETING THE PRESIDENT

Like Ernie, President Ronald Reagan also broadcast games through re-creation. When Reagan was a sports announcer at WHO Des Moines, he broadcast games of the Cubs and White Sox but never left Des Moines.

ANDRE J. JACKSON

SPELLING OUT OUR LOVE

From left, Christine Jonasz-Wofford of Canton, Greg Royteck of Toledo and Brian Derengowski of Detroit spell "Ernie" in his memory at Comerica Park.

DIANE WEISS

WARM GREETINGS

Tigers president and general manager Dave Dombrowski greets mourners as they pay their respects. "It's a very touching moment for the Tigers and the Harwell family and the fans," Dombrowski said.

DIANE WEISS

HEADING HOME

Fans line up and share their condolences as Ernie Harwell lies at rest during a public viewing at Comerica Park on May 6, 2010. The viewing started at 7 a.m., and one person was in line just before midnight the previous day.

ANDRE J. JACKSON

A DAY OF EMOTION

John Craft of Berkley mourns outside the main gate during the public viewing. Ernie is believed to be the first person to lie in repose at a Tigers ballpark.

ANDRE J. JACKSON

AT THE HEART OF MANY

Ernie's casket during the public viewing was placed next to his statue inside the main entrance at Comerica Park. Several photos of him through the years were on display.

 Ernie

MILITARY MAN

While in the U.S. Marine Corps in 1942-46, Ernie was a writer and sports editor for Leatherneck, the Marine magazine. In 1945, he visited the Washington Senators' wartime spring training home in Maryland to write an article about Bert Shepard, a war hero trying out with the team.

COURTESY OF THE ERNIE HARWELL SPORTS COLLECTION, DETROIT PUBLIC LIBRARY

THE EARLY YEARS

SEPT. 14, 1968: *TIGERS PITCHER DENNY MCLAIN WINS HIS 30TH GAME OF THE SEASON:*

"A MAN ON FIRST AND A MAN ON THIRD, ONE MAN DOWN, 2-2 THE COUNT ON WILLIE HORTON. HERE'S THE SET BY SEGUI, HERE'S THE PITCH. SWUNG ON — A DRIVE TO LEFT, THAT'LL BE THE BALLGAME! IT'S OVER THE HEAD OF GOSGER! MCLAIN WINS HIS 30TH! HERE COMES CASH IN TO SCORE! WILLIE HORTON HAS SINGLED AND THE BALLGAME IS OVER. THE TIGERS WIN IT, 5-4. DENNY MCLAIN IS ONE OF THE FIRST OUT OF THE DUGOUT, RACING OUT, AND HORTON IS MOBBED AS THE TIGERS COME FROM BEHIND AND MCLAIN HAS HIS 30TH VICTORY OF THE 1968 SEASON."

COURTESY OF THE GARY SPICER COLLECTION

YOUNG ERNIE

Ernie grew up in Washington, Ga. He was the third son of Gray and Helen Harwell. As a youth, he had a paper route for the Atlanta Georgian that included the residence of "Gone with the Wind" author Margaret Mitchell. In baseball, he played second base and had big-league dreams.

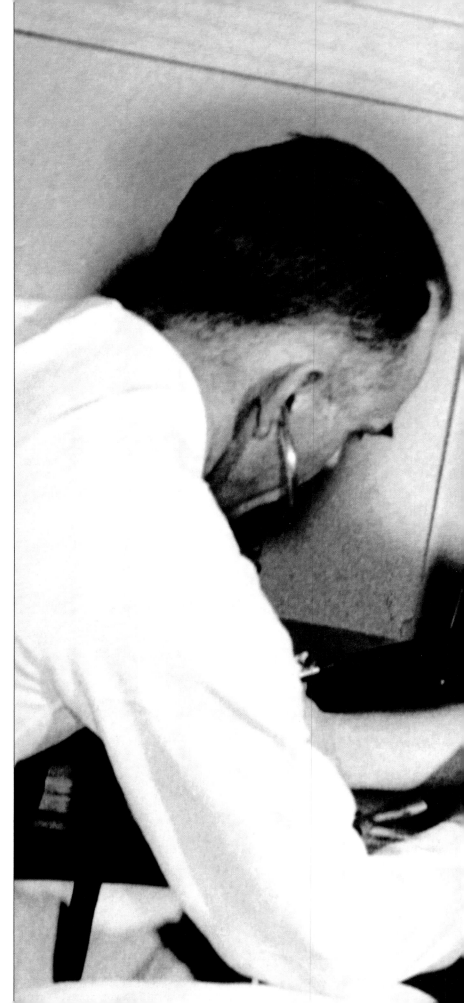

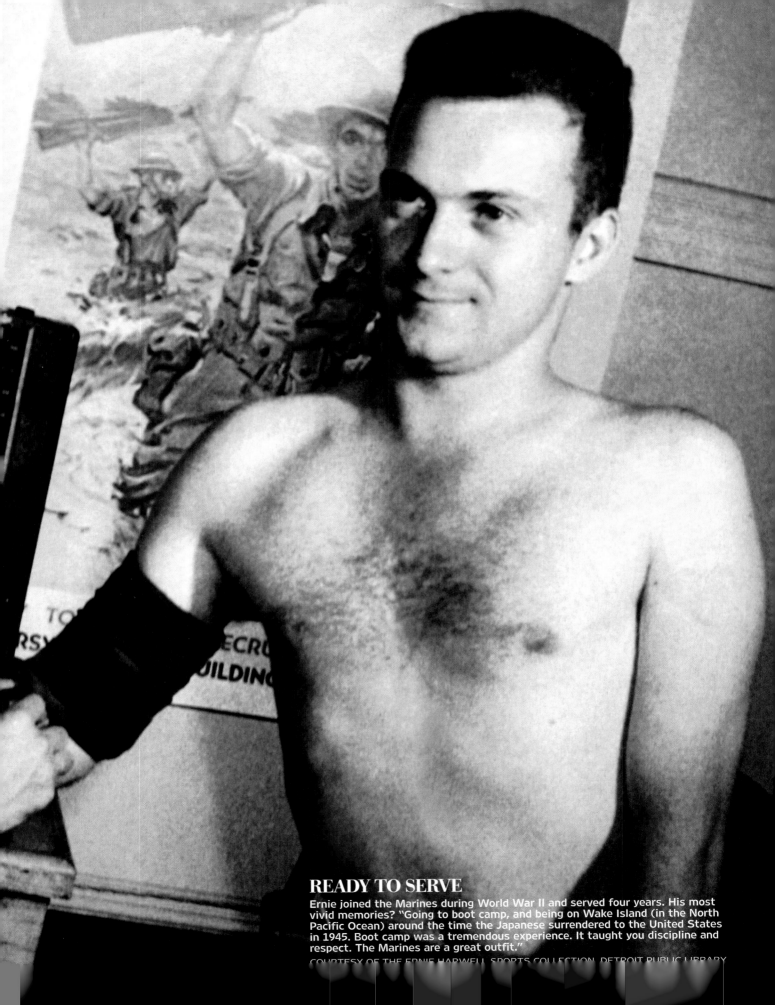

READY TO SERVE

Ernie joined the Marines during World War II and served four years. His most vivid memories? "Going to boot camp, and being on Wake Island (in the North Pacific Ocean) around the time the Japanese surrendered to the United States in 1945. Boot camp was a tremendous experience. It taught you discipline and respect. The Marines are a great outfit."

COURTESY OF THE ERNIE HARWELL SPORTS COLLECTION, DETROIT PUBLIC LIBRARY

A veteran of radio

BY JOHN LOWE

William Earnest Harwell was older than the profession that made him famous. When he was born on Jan. 25, 1918, commercial radio was a few years from its launch. If fans in those days wanted to know about baseball games, they either attended them or read about them in newspapers. The written word was, by far, the dominant means of communication.

Harwell was born in Washington, Ga., a rural town where his father ran a furniture store. When Harwell was 5, the store failed, and the family moved to Atlanta.

Young Ernie Harwell had a speech impediment. He corrected it by taking weekly lessons with an elocution teacher named Margaret Lackland. Among the works she had him read aloud was a poem called "The House by the Side of the Road." Harwell didn't forget that poem. In his broadcasts, he often said that a batter who took a third strike had "stood there like the house by the side of the road."

Harwell got his first broadcasting job in 1940, when he was 22 and a student at Emory University in Atlanta. He became the lone sportscaster for local station WSB, and he did 15-minute reports twice a night.

"All the time I was at WSB, I dreamed of doing baseball play-by-play," Harwell wrote. "That was my first love."

The same year that he began broadcasting, Harwell met Lulu Tankersley, a Kentucky native attending college in Georgia. They were married in that now-romanticized time just before America's entry into World War II: the summer of 1941.

That December, Japan bombed Pearl Harbor, and America was at war. In 1942, Harwell enlisted in the Marines. The next year, he got a brief, first chance at baseball broadcasting. He was stationed in Atlanta, doing public relations work for the Marines when Atlanta Crackers president Earl Mann retained him to do the club's games. Harwell recalled that he did no more than a handful because of his obligations to the Marines.

Later in the war, Harwell went to the Pacific and wrote for the Marines publication Leatherneck. He traveled as far as China.

The war ended in the late summer of 1945, and on Opening Day in 1946, Harwell learned he had gotten the job as the Crackers' full-time play-by-play announcer. More than 50 years later, he called it "the most important day of my career." Ernie Harwell was in baseball broadcasting to stay.

AT THE MIKE IN YEAR 1

During his senior year at Emory University, Ernie landed his first broadcasting job in May 1940 with radio station WSB in Atlanta. He interviewed sports celebrities such as Babe Ruth, Connie Mack and Jack Dempsey.

COURTESY OF THE ERNIE HARWELL SPORTS COLLECTION, DETROIT PUBLIC LIBRARY

THE WSB STAFF

At 22, Ernie did 15-minute reports twice a night during his first broadcasting job at WSB in Atlanta in 1940. He was the sports director on a one-man sports staff in 1940-42.

COURTESY OF THE ERNIE HARWELL SPORTS COLLECTION, DETROIT PUBLIC LIBRARY

COURTESY OF THE ERNIE HARWELL SPORTS COLLECTION, DETROIT PUBLIC LIBRARY

THE FEW, THE PROUD ...

Ernie joined the U.S. Marine Corps in July 1942 and served stateside and overseas until January 1946.

COURTESY OF THE ERNIE HARWELL SPORTS COLLECTION, DETROIT PUBLIC LIBRARY

A FEW GOOD MEN (AND WOMEN)

Ernie, fourth from right, took a break from radio during his four years in the Marines. He did manage to see his first game at Yankee Stadium while on leave — the 1943 World Series opener against the St. Louis Cardinals. Being in uniform, he got to move to the front of the ticket line that stretched two or three blocks around the stadium.

"My father took me to the Cubs-Tigers World Series in 1935, which the Tigers won. I remember writing to the newspapers in Detroit to get all their accounts of the games. I was a baseball fan since I can remember."

ERNIE HARWELL, *ON BEING A BASEBALL FAN*

LEGENDARY MEETINGS

Ernie Harwell is probably the only person you could meet in 2009 who met Connie Mack, Babe Ruth, Ty Cobb and Ted Williams — and had a great story to go along with it.

BABE RUTH

As a 12-year-old in 1930, Harwell met Ruth when the Yankees came to Atlanta for an exhibition game. Harwell didn't have any paper for the Babe to autograph, and the outcome of that episode became the title of one of Ernie's books, "The Babe Signed My Shoe."

CONNIE MACK

At the dawn of his radio career in Atlanta in 1940, Harwell interviewed a man born during the Civil War. It was Mack, the Philadelphia Athletics manager since 1901. Mack recounted in detail for Harwell how Christy Mathewson of the New York Giants threw three shutouts against Mack's A's in the 1905 World Series.

TY COBB

As a broadcaster in the 1940s and 1950s, Harwell got to know Cobb. Theirs was a relationship between two Georgians — one who had taken over Detroit baseball by the storm of his playing talent, and one who would take it over by the pleasing, flowing river of his words. Cobb wasn't known for making friends, but Harwell says that Cobb "was very good to me, he really was."

TED WILLIAMS

Williams once asked Harwell to go over a speech with him that he had written. That tells you something about the respect Williams had for how Harwell used words. It also shows you how long Harwell lasted in baseball since the request was made when Harwell was broadcasting for the Baltimore Orioles — before he began his 42-year run with the Tigers.

BY JOHN LOWE

A GOOD READ

Ernie reads the Baltimore News-Post. Harwell worked in Baltimore in 1954-59 as the Orioles broadcaster before leaving to join the Tigers.

COURTESY OF THE ERNIE HARWELL SPORTS COLLECTION, DETROIT PUBLIC LIBRARY

JUST YOUR TYPE

While in the Marines, Ernie augmented his $78-a-month salary by freelancing. In 1943, he sold an article to the Detroit Free Press about Paul Richards, the Atlanta Crackers manager, returning to the big leagues as a catcher. He also wrote a Saturday Evening Post article on Ty Cobb and sold pieces to Esquire, Reader's Digest, Parade and other publications.

COURTESY OF THE ERNIE HARWELL SPORTS COLLECTION, DETROIT PUBLIC LIBRARY

COURTESY OF THE ERNIE HARWELL SPORTS COLLECTION, DETROIT PUBLIC LIBRARY

BOOT CAMP TIME

Ernie attended Marine boot camp at Parris Island, S.C. About 19,000 recruits are trained at Parris Island each year.

YOUNG LOVEBIRDS

Ernie Harwell and Lulu Tankersley met in 1940 and married the next year. Lulu, a Kentucky native attending college in Georgia, was introduced to Ernie by one of his fraternity brothers at Emory University.

COURTESY OF THE ERNIE HARWELL SPORTS COLLECTION, DETROIT PUBLIC LIBRARY

THE WAR IN JAPAN

The streets in Japan were busy during the era of World War II. Ernie spent time in the North Pacific during his time with the Marines.

COURTESY OF THE ERNIE HARWELL SPORTS COLLECTION, DETROIT PUBLIC LIBRARY

"My feeling was always I was a reporter — it was a prerogative of the fan to root, and not mine. . . . Nobody is going to approve of every style. If you please everybody, maybe you don't have any style. I started out hoping I could do it in the minor leagues. I never thought I would last seven decades. I love this game."

HARWELL, *UPON ANNOUNCING THAT 2002 WOULD BE HIS FINAL SEASON OF BROADCASTING*

A WORD FROM OUR SPONSOR

Gunther Beer sponsored the Orioles during Ernie's final three years in Baltimore (1957-59). Ernie originally thought Gunther would not retain him in 1957, but when discussing his status with a Gunther representative at a Baltimore Chinese restaurant, a miracle happened. The waiter happened to have a petition to keep Ernie as the Orioles announcer — without knowing Ernie was at the table. It left a lasting impression on the Gunther representative, and Ernie kept his job.

COURTESY OF THE ERNIE HARWELL SPORTS COLLECTION, DETROIT PUBLIC LIBRARY

HOME AT THE PARK
Ernie worked more than 8,500 radio and television broadcasts between 1948 and 2002: "I started out hoping I could do it in the minor leagues. I never thought I would last seven decades. I love this game."

COURTESY OF THE ERNIE HARWELL SPORTS COLLECTION, DETROIT PUBLIC LIBRARY

IN THE BOOTH

CALLS FROM *THE VOICE OF SUMMER*

SEPT. 17, 1968: *TIGERS CLINCH THEIR FIRST BERTH IN THE WORLD SERIES SINCE 1945:*

"WELL, THIS BIG CROWD HERE READY TO BREAK LOOSE. THREE MEN ON, TWO OUT, GAME TIED, 1–1, IN THE NINTH INNING. MCDANIEL CHECKING HIS SIGN WITH JAKE GIBBS. THE TALL RIGHT-HANDER READY TO GO TO WORK AGAIN. AND THE WINDUP, AND THE PITCH. HE SWINGS — A LINE SHOT, BASE HIT, RIGHTFIELD! THE TIGERS WIN IT! HERE COMES KALINE TO SCORE! AND IT'S ALL OVER! DON WERT SINGLES! THE TIGERS MOB DON. KALINE HAS SCORED, THE FANS ARE STREAMING ON THE FIELD, AND THE TIGERS HAVE WON THEIR FIRST PENNANT SINCE NINETEEN-HUNDRED-AND-45! LET'S LISTEN TO THE BEDLAM HERE AT TIGER STADIUM!"

NEW YORK MINUTE

Ernie broadcast New York Giants baseball games as the No. 2 announcer for WMCA-AM (570) from 1950-53. After that, he joined the Baltimore Orioles in 1954.

EYES ON MOTOWN

In 1967 — Ernie's eighth year with the Tigers — Detroit saw its baseball team blow the American League pennant on the final day. The Tigers were denied a share of the pennant with Boston by losing the second game of a doubleheader to California. The 8-5 loss ended when Dick McAuliffe hit into a double play — the only one McAuliffe hit into all season. Ernie said missing the post-season that year was the biggest regret of his career.

COURTESY OF THE ERNIE HARWELL SPORTS COLLECTION, DETROIT PUBLIC LIBRARY

COURTESY OF THE ERNIE HARWELL SPORTS COLLECTION, DETROIT PUBLIC LIBRARY

"The greatest thing an announcer can have is longevity. It's sort of like an old bedroom slipper. It's easier to slip on than a new shoe."

HARWELL, *ON HIS APPEAL IN DETROIT*

King of the mike

BY JOHN LOWE

By Ernie Harwell's third season broadcasting Crackers games in Atlanta, 1948, he had attracted the interest of Branch Rickey, the renowned executive who ran the Brooklyn Dodgers. To get Harwell's services, Rickey traded minor league catcher Cliff Dapper to Atlanta. Crackers owner Earl Mann wanted Dapper to be his club's manager, and he was willing to give up his broadcaster to get him.

Thus, thanks to perhaps the only broadcaster-player trade in baseball history, Ernie Harwell broke into the majors as a broadcaster in August 1948 with the Dodgers. After a year as the No. 3 broadcaster for the Dodgers, he became the No. 2 announcer with the crosstown New York Giants. To replace Harwell, the Dodgers hired a young announcer recently out of Fordham University, Vin Scully.

Fifty years later, as the 21st Century arrived, Harwell and Scully were still on the air. Scully never left the Dodgers. Harwell spent four seasons with the Giants, then 1954-59 with the Baltimore Orioles before he was hired by the Detroit Tigers in 1960. Harwell teamed with George Kell for four years before Kell left after the 1963 season. By then Harwell had become prominent enough that NBC radio assigned him to the World Series.

After three more partners, Harwell was joined in the Tigers' radio booth by Paul Carey in 1973. Harwell said Carey had the best voice of any of his partners. Carey's baritone mixed beautifully with Harwell's sweet Southern tones, and the two became a memorable combination for the next 19 seasons. Carey had decided he would retire following the '91 season. Then Tigers management decided not to retain Harwell, either.

Harwell missed the 1992 season, but returned in '93 as part of a team with Rick Rizzs and Bob Rathbun. In '94, Harwell left radio and began a five-year run on Tigers telecasts. Harwell returned to the radio full time in 1999 and broadcasted through the 2002 season before retiring.

Harwell had the folksiness to present the game's local sandlot feel, and the knowledge and respect to convey its history and grandeur. That made him a friendly, informed neighbor — the most interesting kind of company to have on the radio every night of the baseball season.

A VOICE ALWAYS HEARD

In 55 seasons of broadcasting big-league baseball, Ernie missed two games, neither because of his health. One was for his brother's funeral in 1968 and another was for his introduction into the National Sportscasters and Sportswriters Association Hall of Fame in 1989.

COURTESY OF THE ERNIE HARWELL SPORTS COLLECTION, DETROIT PUBLIC LIBRARY

AT THE POLO GROUNDS

Ernie works a New York Giants game at the Polo Grounds in 1952. One year earlier, Ernie called Bobby Thomson's "Shot Heard 'Round the World" in the National League pennant play-off game.

COURTESY OF THE ERNIE HARWELL SPORTS COLLECTION, DETROIT PUBLIC LIBRARY

LOOK OF A WINNER

The glasses may have changed, but Ernie remained much the same from his major league debut to his final broadcast.

ALL PHOTOS COURTESY OF THE ERNIE HARWELL SPORTS COLLECTION, DETROIT PUBLIC LIBRARY

1954

1955

1956

1961

"I'd like to be remembered as someone who showed up for the job. I consider myself a worker. I love what I do. If I had my time over again, I'd probably do it for nothing."

1964

1990

1980

1970

ROBERT KOZLOFF

COUNTDOWN AT THE CORNER

Ernie reacts to a player on the field between innings of a September game between the Tigers and Royals in 1999 at Tiger Stadium. Only two more games would be played at The Corner.

MICHIGAN & TRUMBULL

Shown here in 1979, Ernie enjoyed one of the best views in the house during his 39 years of broadcasting games at Tiger Stadium on radio and television.

SCOTT ECCKER

CALLS FROM *THE VOICE OF SUMMER*

AUG. 2, 1981: *ERNIE HARWELL EMBLAZONED HIS COMPELLING DUAL SENSE OF THE GAME OF BASEBALL INTO THE WRITTEN RECORD IN 1955, WHEN HE PENNED THESE WORDS FOR THE SPORTING NEWS THAT HE LATER INCLUDED IN HIS 1981 NATIONAL BASEBALL HALL OF FAME SPEECH:*

"BASEBALL IS THE PRESIDENT TOSSING OUT THE FIRST BALL OF THE SEASON AND A SCRUBBY SCHOOLBOY PLAYING CATCH WITH HIS DAD ON A MISSISSIPPI FARM. ... IN BASEBALL, DEMOCRACY SHINES ITS CLEAREST. THE ONLY RACE THAT MATTERS IS THE RACE TO THE BAG. THE CREED IS THE RULE BOOK AND COLOR, MERELY SOMETHING TO DISTINGUISH ONE TEAM'S UNIFORM FROM ANOTHER'S."

COURTESY OF THE ERNIE HARWELL SPORTS COLLECTION, DETROIT PUBLIC LIBRARY

ERNIE AND PAUL

Ernie and Paul Carey, right, formed the Tigers' radio broadcast team in 1973-91. They compiled a streak of 2,551 consecutive games broadcast together before each missed a game in April 1989.

A perfect pairing

BY JOE LAPOINTE

One smokes, the other doesn't. One rises with the morning sun; the other might get to bed an hour or two before dawn's early light. One goes for long walks; the other can't motivate himself to exercise.

One is from the South, the other from the North.

One speaks in a baritone, sometimes rising to tenor.

The other also is a baritone, sometimes dropping to bass.

And yet, when it comes to Tigers baseball, they seem to speak with one voice.

Ernie and Paul. Harwell and Carey. They're a team. Like Burns and Allen, Batman and Robin, Whitaker and Trammell, peanut butter and jelly.

"Thank-ya mis-tah Paul Carey . . ."

They're there, in your car, in the dashboard, while you drive along the expressway on a drizzly April day. You hear them at the beach, booming from some guy's blaster box on a hot afternoon in August. Or late on a cool, crisp September night, near the end of a pennant race, faint and muffled, from under the pillow in the kids' bedrooms upstairs.

"Ernie, it looked as if the ball ricocheted down there in the corner and then it seemed to . . ."

Harwell and Carey were together longer than many Tigers fans have been married, longer than some have been alive.

Harwell is the one from the South, a native Georgian who doesn't smoke, falls asleep easily after a game, reaches a tenor pitch when he gets excited, takes long walks in the morning with Tigers manager Sparky Anderson and has been married since 1941.

Carey is the worrying, nervous smoker with the voice that sounds like God talking to Noah in the old Bill Cosby record.

Why does their personal chemistry work so well?

"Basically, what it comes down to is we have different personalities," Carey says. "And I think that's why it works well. I'm a fretter and a worrier. I like the responsibility of the small details. I think Ernie does not. Ernie would like to come in and enjoy the overall atmosphere of the ballpark. Ernie feels that everything is going to come out all right."

They never had an argument.

"I don't think anybody could ever get mad at Ernie Harwell," Carey says.

ERIC SEALS

ERNIE AND JIM

Jim Price, left, and Ernie dress warm for the February spring training opener against the Pirates in 2002 in Lakeland, Fla. It marked the first game of Ernie's final season as a Tigers broadcaster.

"There's a little tinge of sadness. But I have no regrets. It's been a great ride for me. As Satchel Paige said, 'Don't ever look back.' God has something good in store for me, and I look forward to my next adventure."

HARWELL, *ON HIS FIRST BROADCASTING GOOD-BYE IN 1993*

OVER THE YEARS

A look at Ernie Harwell's radio partners through the years in Detroit:

1960-63
George Kell for WKMH

1964
Bob Scheffing for WJR

1965-66
Gene Osborn for WJR

1967-72
Ray Lane for WJR

1973-91
Paul Carey for WJR

1993
Rick Rizzs and Bob Rathbun for WJR

1999
Jim Price for WJR

2000
Dan Dickerson and Price for WJR

2001-02
Dickerson and Price for WXYT

CELEBRATE GOOD TIMES

Ernie reacts to a good play by the Tigers in 1979. Paul Carey is in the background. The two worked together longer than any other Tigers radio broadcast team.

SCOTT ECCKER

Ernie

COURTESY OF THE ERNIE HARWELL SPORTS COLLECTION, DETROIT PUBLIC LIBRARY

ERNIE AND RAY

Ray Lane, left, and Ernie formed the Tigers' radio broadcast team in 1967-72. Lane left to become sports anchor at Channel 2 but later said he regretted the decision. "I look back now and say, 'Why did I do it?' " Lane said in 1990.

COURTESY OF THE ERNIE HARWELL SPORTS COLLECTION, DETROIT PUBLIC LIBRARY

ERNIE AND GEORGE

George Kell, left, and Ernie formed the Tigers' radio/television broadcast team in 1960-63. After a one-year hiatus, Kell moved to Tigers television in 1965-96. It was Kell who worked with Ernie in Baltimore and helped persuade the Tigers to hire Ernie in 1960.

THREE'S COMPANY

From left, Chuck Thompson, Bailey Goss and Ernie worked Baltimore Orioles games together for radio and television in 1955-56. Thompson went on to become a legendary broadcaster who called Orioles games for parts of five decades.

COURTESY OF THE ERNIE HARWELL SPORTS COLLECTION, DETROIT PUBLIC LIBRARY

ALL SHE WROTE

Ernie watches as the Royals and Tigers play the final game at Tiger Stadium on Sept. 27, 1999. Detroit won, 8-2, behind Robert Fick's eighth-inning grand slam.

GABRIEL B. TAIT

FREE PRESS FILE PHOTO

ONE OF THE BOYS

Ernie chats with, from left, John Wockenfuss, Aurelio Rodriguez and Milt May inside the Tigers' locker room during the 1970s.

VOICE OF THE TIGERS

SEPT. 27, 1999: *THE FINAL MOMENTS OF TIGER STADIUM:*

"WHAT A THRILL! WHAT A SENSATION HERE IN THE FINAL GAME. OUTSIDE, AND THE COUNT GOES 2-2. BELTRAN HAS SINGLED, SINGLED, DOUBLED AND WALKED. HE'S GOT A PERFECT NIGHT. TIGERS LEAD IT, 8-2, TWO DOWN IN THE NINTH INNING. JONES IS READY. HE DELIVERS. HERE'S A SWING, AND A MISS — THE GAME'S OVER! AND TIGER STADIUM IS NO MORE. THE FINAL SCORE, THE TIGERS 8, AND THE ROYALS 2."

A FEW MINUTES AFTER 8: *HOME PLATE WAS PLACED IN THE TIGERS' NEW HOME, COMERICA PARK, BOOED AT EVERY MENTION. THE PLAYERS THREW BASEBALLS INTO THE STANDS. THE LIGHTS TURNED OFF. THE FANS LEANED OVER THE RAILING, SCOOPING UP DIRT WITH PLASTIC CUPS. HARWELL SAID FAREWELL, GOLDEN VOICE BREAKING:*

"TONIGHT, WE SAY GOOD-BYE ... BUT WE WILL NOT FORGET. MOMENTS LIKE THIS SHALL LIVE ON FOREVER."

GREATS OF THE '80S

Ernie joined Tigers greats Alan Trammell, left, and Kirk Gibson on stage at Fries Auditorium at the Grosse Pointe War Memorial during a charity event in 2009. The guests knew the ballplayers would be there, but Ernie was a surprise when he entered the stage during a story about him.

MANDI WRIGHT

CLASSY TRAM

Ernie knew Alan Trammell well from his 20 seasons as a player and three years as a manager for the Tigers. "There has never been a classier guy in baseball," Ernie wrote in a Free Press column.

COURTESY OF THE GARY SPICER COLLECTION

COURTESY OF THE ERNIE HARWELL SPORTS COLLECTION, DETROIT PUBLIC LIBRARY

FUN WITH PHIL

Ernie and another former Tigers manager, Phil Garner, don sombreros. Garner was skipper for two seasons (2000-01) and six games (2002) before he was fired. He went on to manage the Astros in a World Series.

ERIC SEALS

MORE GOOD TIMES

Ernie shares a laugh with Tigers great Willie Horton, left, and Judge Damon Keith at an event honoring Horton during the Soul Food Luncheon in Detroit in 2008.

HONORING THE GREATS

Ernie tips his cap during a ceremony that honored Tigers greats Lou Whitaker, left, and Alan Trammell before the 1997 spring training opener in Lakeland, Fla. Whitaker retired in '95, Trammell in '96.

JULIAN H. GONZALEZ

Detroit dialed in

BY HEATH J MERIWETHER

For me and my family, Ernie Harwell's voice on the radio became a connection to our home and a reminder of Detroit's baseball history.

It's a connection made in millions of different ways by generations of Tigers listeners.

His reverence for language comes from his mother, a great reader, but more specifically his stint as a sports copy editor at the Atlanta Constitution while in high school and in college at Emory University.

"Reading copy and writing headlines taught me a lot about brevity and clarity and unity," he said.

He learned how to edit verbose writers and make their stories more compelling — a craft he naturally brings to his own writing and storytelling.

His father taught him baseball and became Ernie's imaginary audience as a broadcaster. His dad developed multiple sclerosis in his 30s and though he lived into his 70s, was housebound and looked forward to broadcasts of the minor league Atlanta Crackers.

"The listeners' imagination is the greatest instrument a radio announcer has," Harwell said.

BY CHARLIE VINCENT

He is the voice of baseball in Detroit. Dulcet, friendly, melodious.

Every day he is the same, a rock of stability.

"Hello, everybody, this is Ernie Harwell . . ." and you are no longer in your living room, you are in Exhibition Stadium or someplace like it.

He is the voice of baseball, the voice of spring, the voice of optimism.

Ernie Harwell probably could have broadcast World War II without sounding distressed. "Hello, everybody, this is Ernie Harwell and it's a lovely day here in the foxhole ... "

He has described mammoth home runs and monumental victories, dozens of Opening Days and heady World Series championships.

To most Detroiters, Ernie Harwell is as close as they ever get to the Tigers. He doesn't wear a uniform or swing a bat, but he is a part of the team as surely as Jack Morris or Lou Whitaker or Chet Lemon. He has been a Tiger longer than any of them.

COURTESY OF THE ERNIE HARWELL SPORTS COLLECTION, DETROIT PUBLIC LIBRARY

WITH THE BIG SLUGGER

Shown here in 1995, Ernie made the famous call five years earlier when Cecil Fielder became the second Tiger with 50 homers: "And it's a home run for Cecil Fielder — No. 50. Now Cecil's happy." He ended up with 51 in joining Hank Greenberg, who hit 58 in 1938.

A LYRICAL TOUCH

Ernie Harwell had dozens of songs published — some of them recorded by artists such as Mitch Ryder, Homer and Jethro and B.J. Thomas. Harwell wrote a song called "Tiger, Tiger" for the 1984 pennant race. Dan Yessian, a local songwriter and jingle producer, set it to music. Mark Bucchare sang it. The song hit local record stores and received play on Detroit-area radio stations.

"TIGER, TIGER" LYRICS

(CHORUS)
Tiger, Tiger Baseball Team, reaching for that pennant dream.
Tiger, Tiger Baseball Team, reaching for that pennant dream.
C'Mon, Tigers, Detroit Tigers, My Baseball Team.

(FIRST VERSE)
Soon we'll hear the cheers or boos,
Telling us if they win or lose.
Know for certain when they score,
We're gonna hear those Tigers roar.

(CHORUS)

(SECOND VERSE)
They got tradition on their side,
Fantastic fans and hometown pride.
Greenberg, Cobb and Kaline, too,
Tiger heroes who come through.

(CHORUS)

ARIZONA FOURSOME

From left, Brooks Robinson, Woody Woodruff, Ernie and Jim Archer stop for a photo in 1956 during spring training in Scottsdale, Ariz. "Ernie's a wonderful person and great for baseball," Archer said in early 2010.

COURTESY OF THE ERNIE HARWELL SPORTS COLLECTION, DETROIT PUBLIC LIBRARY

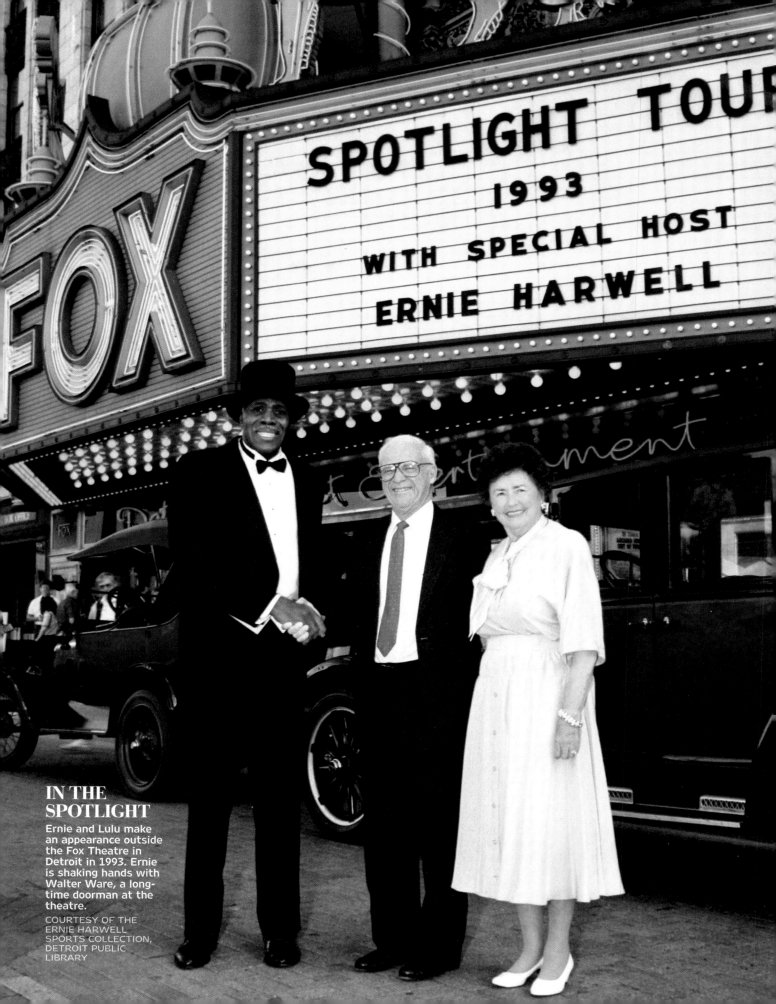

IN THE SPOTLIGHT

Ernie and Lulu make an appearance outside the Fox Theatre in Detroit in 1993. Ernie is shaking hands with Walter Ware, a long-time doorman at the theatre.

COURTESY OF THE ERNIE HARWELL SPORTS COLLECTION, DETROIT PUBLIC LIBRARY

STATE OF GLORY

OCT. 5, 1984: *THE TIGERS SWEEP KANSAS CITY IN THE ALCS AT TIGER STADIUM:*

"BALL ONE THE COUNT ON MOTLEY. HERE'S THE PITCH. MOTLEY SWINGS — HERE'S A POP FOUL OFF OF THIRD. IT MAY BE THE PENNANT! CASTILLO HAS IT, AND THE TIGERS HAVE WON THE AMERICAN LEAGUE PENNANT, THEIR FIRST SINCE 1968. WILLIE HERNANDEZ HUGGED BY HIS TEAMMATES! THE POLICE ARE TRYING TO KEEP THE SPECTATORS OFF THE FIELD! SOME HAVE BROKEN FROM THE CENTERFIELD AREA! AND THE TIGERS ARE CELEBRATING THEIR NINTH AMERICAN LEAGUE PENNANT TONIGHT HERE AT THE CORNER OF MICHIGAN AND TRUMBULL! WHAT A NIGHT THIS HAS BEEN!"

COURTESY OF THE NATIONAL BASEBALL HALL OF FAME

HALL OF FAME HONOREE

Ernie receives the Ford C. Frick Award from Ralph Kiner at the National Baseball Hall of Fame in 1981. The award is given annually for excellence in baseball broadcasting. Ernie would normally not be able to attend the ceremony because of his broadcast duties, but there were no games that day because of the baseball strike.

" 'Are you going to Cooperstown for the induction ceremonies?' ... And the answer is, 'No, I'm not going.' ... I don't want to give up a broadcast. The first rule in radio is: 'Don't leave your microphone. You might lose your job to the guy who replaces you.' "

HARWELL, *WHEN ASKED IN 2001 WHETHER HE WOULD ATTEND THE HALL OF FAME CEREMONY*

BRIAN KAUFMAN

ANN ARBOR HONOREE

Ernie receives an honorary doctorate of humane letters from University of Michigan president Mary Sue Coleman during the spring commencement ceremony in 2008.

MAIL CALL
Stacks of mail from well-wishers sit on a coffee table at Ernie's Novi home in 2009. Ernie received more than 10,000 letters and cards after revealing he had cancer in September 2009.

A man for Michigan

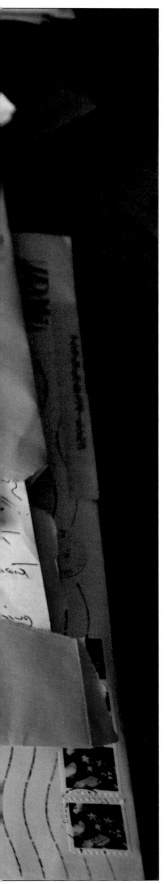

MANDI WRIGHT

BY ROCHELLE RILEY

You never know how many lives you've touched until people show you by their actions. When you're Ernie Harwell, they tell you in more than 8,500 cards and letters when they hear that you're sick.

When you're Ernie Harwell, everybody, including sports superstars, wants to interview you. Harwell did Frank Deford's HBO special and a Bob Costas interview. Even at 91, he was trying to grant 23 other requests.

But that's Harwell. A gentleman, a legend, a humble servant of the sport of baseball. His idea of slowing down means skipping parades or marathons.

That's why, when you're Ernie Harwell, thousands cheer as you stand on the field at Comerica Park.

And that's why the announcement that Harwell, the beloved Detroit Tigers broadcaster, has inoperable cancer moved a Grandville firefighter to action.

Kevin McNutt, a father of four boys

JULIAN H. GONZALEZ

BACK FOR MORE

A fan welcomes Ernie for another season on Opening Day in 1997. It marked his 50th season of broadcasting Major League Baseball. He did the game for Channel 50 with help from George Kell and Al Kaline.

and "big Tigers fan," decided to honor Harwell by starting a Facebook page for a cause: to change the name of Comerica Park to Ernie Harwell Field at Comerica Park.

From a firefighter in a west Michigan city who loves Detroit to a Southern tomboy-turned-city girl who loves the Tigers as if I'd been here all my life, we all want to honor Ernie Harwell.

A MAN OF THE PEOPLE

Free Press readers and Ernie's friends share their stories:

REV. GREGORY GIBBONS, LIVONIA

"Ernie Harwell is the epitome of class. He is a fine Christian gentleman whom I have known for almost 20 years, and my life is so much greater for knowing him and his beautiful wife, Lulu. There are very few people in this world that have absolutely no enemies, only friends. Ernie Harwell is one of them."

EUSEBIA AQUINO-HUGHES, DETROIT

"Back in the winter of 1988, I was working as a nurse when I was told I had cancer. I knew I had to go through chemotherapy. I wanted to die just to get away from the depression and bone pain that comes from chemo. My husband got me a radio, and I started to listen to the Tigers games and concentrate on Ernie Harwell's soft, easy-does-it voice. Harwell pulled me through that painful year. The sound of his voice gave me the positive charge I needed to face the next day. He made each game sound as if I were batting a home run when it came to chemo. He also made me laugh with his wacky humor. His voice was better than pain medication for me."

ROBERT DENSTEDT, CANTON

"Listening to him broadcast Tigers games as my father and I listened are memories I'll never forget. The 'Long gone!' I used to hear him say after a Tiger home run will always be in my mind. When all is said and done, this man will be a Michigan icon."

CLARK AND BARB REID, NOVI

"As Ernie Harwell's neighbors, what a pleasure it has been to know his happy smile and his zest for living. Genuine nice guy, friend to everyone."

THOMAS MYERS, MIDLAND

"Nothing could bring sunshine to a rainy Michigan day better than Harwell's voice from a far-away sunny ballpark. Also, there was no better proof that, yes, spring would return to Michigan than to hear that first spring training game from Florida."

BERNARD JUOZAPAITIS, DETROIT

"Back in the '60s and '70s, I lived in one of the roughest neighborhoods in Detroit. As my father sat on the porch and listened to Ernie Harwell, the roughest young men in the neighborhood as they walked by would stop and sit with my dad for a couple of innings and make small talk about the Tigers and other things. Many times, mortal enemies would sit together on that porch and just forget their differences and enjoy the play-by-play. It was like an oasis that would let these young men forget their troubled lives for a moment."

JERRY BARR, ORLANDO

"I have known Ernie Harwell for 25 years, and he has been the most kind, honest, friendly and knowledgeable man I have known. Once you are introduced to him, he never forgets your name. He is responsible for not only me but for more than a million fans enjoying Detroit Tigers baseball. Thank you, Ernie, and God bless."

JOE MICHNUK, DEARBORN

"Many Michiganders, like me, consider you to be part of our extended family. ... We are grateful you have continued to make us proud with your Hall of Fame approach to life."

TODD WEHRMEYER, HOLLAND

"Many times, I expected to be the 'fan from Holland, Mich.,' who caught a foul ball, and the next day, in my backyard, playing catch with my dad, many times, I was that fan."

PAUL AMICI, HARBOR BEACH

"Regardless of whether the Tigers won or lost, no matter where you were in the world, Harwell brought home closer. Thank you, Mr. Harwell, for all the wonderful years."

JOHN DOBEL, THOUSAND OAKS, CALIF.

"As a child growing up in the '60s in Plymouth, Mr. Harwell taught me baseball. He made the players from Jerry Lumpe to George Thomas come alive every night. He made us understand that there was a history and tradition to the game of baseball that was just as important as the game itself."

MEET AND GREET

The Rev. Bob Shirock greets Ernie at the 2006 grand opening of Oak Pointe Church in Novi. Ernie spoke for 25 minutes as its inaugural preacher.

RICHARD LEE

"When you have a choice to be right or be kind, always be kind."

HARWELL, *ON HIS PHILOSOPHY OF LIFE*

LET'S HAVE A PARADE

Ernie waves to the crowd from his Cinderella float during the 2002 Thanksgiving Day parade in Detroit. Ernie, who served as grand marshal, even got to carry a wand. "It's a great honor to be involved in something that's so much a part of Detroit," he said.

PAUL WARNER/
FREE PRESS
FILE PHOTO

COURTESY OF THE ERNIE HARWELL SPORTS COLLECTION, DETROIT PUBLIC LIBRARY

BASEBALL WONDERLAND

Bronner's Christmas Wonderland honored baseball and Ernie on a parade float. The Tigers' annual winter caravan to promote the team often stopped in Frankenmuth.

ERNIE AND WALLY

Ernie shares the stage with another Michigan legend in Wally Bronner. Bronner founded Bronner's Christmas Wonderland, billed as the world's largest Christmas store, in Frankenmuth in 1945.

FILE PHOTO

Call of fame

DETROIT FREE PRESS EDITORIAL

No matter what, there was the voice.

The Tigers won the World Series, there was the voice. The city went up in flames, there was the voice.

The greats came and went, there was the voice.

For many in Michigan, Ernie Harwell has been synonymous not only with baseball, but with summer. With nostalgia. With kicking back alongside family and friends, enjoying a hot dog, a hot afternoon and, in the good years, a hot team.

There have been too few of the last, especially lately, but Harwell would never complain. He didn't even grouse when a strike threatened to cut short his final season in 2002.

Harwell has written songs, been memorialized on film and had the visitor's broadcasting booth in Cleveland named for him. Like many players, he has been fired, rehired and even traded.

But mostly he has been there, whether the Tigers were at the top of the league or the dregs of the dregs. Day in and day out, he helped Tigers fans see the game even when they could only listen to it. With that voice he could do it all.

CAPTAIN ERNIE

Ernie got to ride in style when he was an honorary captain for the Detroit Lions-Minnesota Vikings game at Detroit's Ford Field in 2009.

MANDI WRIGHT

Ernie

A MAN FOR TWO SEASONS

Ernie chats with Lions owner William Clay Ford Sr. prior to the Lions-Vikings game at Ford Field. Ernie also has some football on his résumé. He called Michigan State games in 1963 and also did the radio broadcast for the Baltimore Colts in their famed 1958 NFL title game with the New York Giants. Before that, he worked for the Giants and several colleges.

MANDI WRIGHT

JULIAN H. GONZALEZ

THE COIN TOSS

Ernie gets ready for the pregame coin toss as a Lions honorary captain. He received a warm ovation from the sellout crowd at Detroit's home opener.

JULIAN H. GONZALEZ

WEARING LIONS BLUE

Ernie puts on a No. 1 Lions jersey with his name on the back. Immediately after putting on Lions' colors, he broke into a dance that resembled a touchdown celebration.

MR. DETROIT MEETS MR. OCTOBER

Whenever Reggie Jackson would see Ernie around the batting cage, he would call him "Hall of Famer." One of Jackson's most memorable homers came when he hit a light tower above the roof in Tiger Stadium during the 1971 All-Star Game. "I think it is still going in outer space," Ernie said.

COURTESY OF THE ERNIE HARWELL SPORTS COLLECTION, DETROIT PUBLIC LIBRARY

ERNIE AND PALS

OCT. 14, 1984: *THE TIGERS TAKE THE WORLD SERIES IN FIVE GAMES OVER SAN DIEGO:*

"ROENICKE OFF THE BAG AT FIRST. THE PITCH, HE (TONY GWYNN) SWINGS — AND THERE'S A FLY BALL TO LEFT, HERE COMES HERNDON, HE'S THERE, HE'S GOT IT — AND THE TIGERS ARE THE CHAMPIONS OF 1984! THEY RACE ON THE FIELD TO MOB HERNANDEZ! THE TIGERS HAVE WON THE WORLD SERIES! THEY ARE THE CHAMPIONS OF THE WORLD IN 1984! THE POLICE ARE TRYING TO CONTAIN THE CROWD HERE NOW. THEY'RE GOING TO HAVE A TOUGH TIME DOING IT. THE TIGERS ARE TRYING TO HEAD FOR THE SAFETY OF THEIR DUGOUT. THE POLICE HAVE CIRCLED THE FIELD, BUT A LOT OF THE EXUBERANT TIGER FANS ARE ON THE FIELD. AND IT WILL TAKE SOME DOING TO GET THEM BACK IN THE STANDS."

COURTESY OF THE ERNIE HARWELL SPORTS COLLECTION, DETROIT PUBLIC LIBRARY

CLEVELAND'S CALL

Indians third baseman Travis Fryman, a former Tiger, presents Ernie with a cap, jersey and plaque during the dedication of the Ernie Harwell Visiting Radio Booth at Jacobs Field before his final broadcast in Cleveland on Aug. 28, 2002.

COURTESY OF THE ERNIE HARWELL SPORTS COLLECTION, DETROIT PUBLIC LIBRARY

HANGIN' WITH JUNIOR

Ernie and Ken Griffey Jr. have some fun before a game at Tiger Stadium. Ernie listed Griffey, Torii Hunter and Curtis Granderson as the best modern-day centerfielders. Ernie's all-time picks: Willie Mays, Mickey Mantle, Joe DiMaggio and Tris Speaker.

NO ORDINARY JOE

Ernie and Joe Torre saw each other often during Torre's 12 years managing the Yankees. Ernie pointed out a little-known fact in a *Free Press* column once: Torre caught Warren Spahn's 300th victory in 1961, but his catcher's mitt has not been seen since he shipped it home after the game.

COURTESY OF THE ERNIE HARWELL SPORTS COLLECTION, DETROIT PUBLIC LIBRARY

ALL-STAR PAIRING

Ernie and Tommy Lasorda say hello in the tunnel at Comerica Park before the 2005 All-Star Game in Detroit. Both have Dodgers ties: Lasorda as a 21-year Hall of Fame manager and Ernie as a team broadcaster in 1948-49.

JULIAN H. GONZALEZ

COURTESY OF THE GARY SPICER COLLECTION

TIME WITH TONY

Gary Spicer, Tony La Russa and Ernie share a moment at Comerica Park. La Russa's teams played the Tigers often during his 18 seasons as an AL manager. "I would watch Alan Trammell take infield practice," La Russa said. "That was like watching McGwire take batting practice."

COURTESY OF THE GARY SPICER COLLECTION

BACK WITH BUCKY

Ernie and Bucky Dent go way back — long before his days as bench coach for the Reds. One of Ernie's most vivid memories of Fenway Park was calling Dent's famous home run that lifted the Yankees past the Red Sox in the 1978 one-game playoff. He later gave Dent a tape of his call on CBS Radio.

COURTESY OF THE ERNIE HARWELL SPORTS COLLECTION, DETROIT PUBLIC LIBRARY

ROGER AND ME

Ernie interviews Roger Clemens in 1991. "Ernie's been a great friend," Clemens said. "We did little parts in the Ty Cobb movie, and he's always been real nice to my extended family that's up this way." Clemens was born in Ohio and has relatives in Michigan.

WITH BIG FRANK

White Sox slugger Frank Thomas once told Ernie he's not a fan of high-scoring games. "I like a medium-type game with a score something like 6-5," Thomas said. "That game will have some interesting flow and a lot of turning points."

COURTESY OF THE ERNIE HARWELL SPORTS
COLLECTION, DETROIT PUBLIC LIBRARY

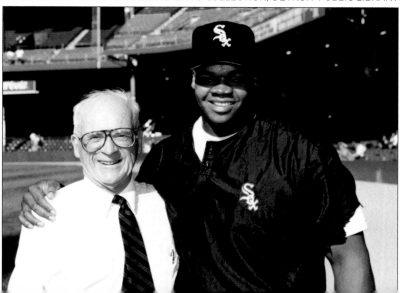

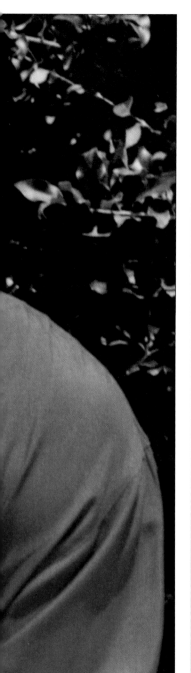

BACK TO ATLANTA

Ernie and Michigan native John Smoltz of the Braves greet each other during game day at Turner Field in Atlanta. In 2002 — Ernie's final season as a Tigers broadcaster — Detroit played three games in Ernie's home state of Georgia.

COURTESY OF THE ERNIE HARWELL SPORTS COLLECTION, DETROIT PUBLIC LIBRARY

A ROYAL MEETING

Ernie and Royals slugger Mike Sweeney share a moment during All-Star Game festivities at Milwaukee in 2002. Before the 2005 All-Star Game in Detroit, Sweeney talked about his Detroit favorites: "My agent always rents out Andiamo's, and I think it's the best Italian restaurant I've ever been to. Also, you can't go to Detroit without hearing Ernie Harwell."

COURTESY OF THE ERNIE HARWELL SPORTS COLLECTION, DETROIT PUBLIC LIBRARY

COURTESY OF THE NATIONAL BASEBALL HALL OF FAME

TALKIN' WITH TED

Ernie first interviewed Hall of Famer Ted Williams, above, in 1942 on WSB Radio in Atlanta. Williams won the Triple Crown that season. "I did a lot of interviews with Ted Williams, and how he loved to talk about hitting," Ernie said.

ICHIRO AND I

Ernie once called Ichiro Suzuki baseball's most fascinating player because of his one-name status, his desire to learn baseball's history and his popularity in Japan. Ernie ranked Al Kaline as the best rightfielder of all time, but put Ichiro at the top of the modern-day list.

BILL EISNER

Rave reviews

During a lifetime love affair with America's pastime, Ernie Harwell has watched some of baseball's greatest players and witnessed many historic moments. From his seat in the booth, Harwell offers his top 10 based on 50-plus years of calling big-league baseball:

BEST PLAYER

"Willie Mays. I saw him make his debut with the Giants in 1951. Mays had the complete tool chest: He could throw, hit and run. He played with spirit and verve. Hank Aaron, Joe DiMaggio and Roberto Clemente were probably the best of the rest."

BEST HITTER

"Ted Williams. The Splendid Splinter was the ultimate student of the game. He possessed great eyesight and combined it with muscle and deft coordination."

BEST PITCHER

"I like Warren Spahn over the long haul. I place him just in front of Sandy Koufax and Bob Gibson. Spahn is the all-time winningest left-hand pitcher in the majors with 363 victories."

BEST OUTFIELDER

"Tiger Al Kaline, who had great instincts in the outfield. He was smooth and grace-ful. Ichiro Suzuki of the Seattle Mariners is a very good rightfielder today."

BEST GUY

"Frank Tanana. I enjoyed being around him a lot. He played for the California Angels, Boston Red Sox, Texas Rangers and Detroit Tigers. He was always fun. Of course, so were Kaline and former Tiger reliever Todd Jones."

BEST TEAM

"I can't pick between the 1949 Brooklyn Dodgers, who had Don Newcombe, Roy Campanella, Pee Wee Reese and Jackie Robinson, and the 1961 New York Yankees, with Mickey Mantle, Roger Maris, Yogi Berra and Whitey Ford. Both were great teams, with pitching and hitting depth."

BEST MOMENT

"I was at the microphone when New York Giant Bobby Thomson hit his playoff home run — 'The Shot Heard 'Round the World' — off Ralph Branca against the Brooklyn Dodgers on Oct. 3, 1951. It was a truly his-toric moment. Kirk Gibson's two upper-deck home runs against the Padres in the 1984 World Series come close."

BEST RESTAURANT

"I always liked Murray's restaurant in down-town Minneapolis. It serves up a great steak. It's just ahead of the lamb at the English Room in Milwaukee and the Maine lobster and tenderloin at Moose's in San Francisco."

BEST BALLPARK

"Tiger Stadium. It had so much history and lore. Seattle's Safeco Field is very good, too."

BEST ERA

"Overall, I think baseball then and now is just as good as it has always been. I was broadcasting in New York, however, in 1949-51. There were probably more good teams during that period than any other time."

BY MIKE BRUDENELL

Ernie

COURTESY OF THE ERNIE HARWELL SPORTS COLLECTION,
DETROIT PUBLIC LIBRARY

BY GEORGE

Ernie said Royals Hall of Famer George Brett is the only
player to ever ask to sit in the radio booth and hear him
broadcast. Brett did it once with Ernie and Paul Carey.

"The main thought
I had was that he
was going to break
the strikeout record.
The no-hitter
kind of sneaked
up on us."

HARWELL, *ON BROADCASTING NOLAN RYAN'S
17-STRIKEOUT NO-HITTER AGAINST THE TIGERS IN 1973*

BILL EISNER

TWO OF A KIND

Ernie and slugger Jim Thome each had their first bobblehead dolls debut in 2001. Thome was overwhelmed and could not wait to tell people, while Ernie felt a little embarrassed. "I was amazed that they would do an old announcer," Ernie said. "That belongs to the players, really."

COURTESY OF THE ERNIE HARWELL SPORTS COLLECTION, DETROIT PUBLIC LIBRARY

ERNIE AND KIRBY

Ernie called Kirby Puckett one of his favorite players. Ernie was impressed with his story of pulling himself out of a Chicago ghetto to become a superstar and by his enthusiasm for the game.

IRON MEN

Ernie and Cal Ripken Jr. each achieved long baseball streaks. Ernie broadcasted 3,215 straight regular-season games between 1968 and 1989. Ripken played in 2,632 consecutive games between 1982 and 1998.

COURTESY OF THE ERNIE HARWELL SPORTS COLLECTION, DETROIT PUBLIC LIBRARY

COURTESY OF THE GARY SPICER COLLECTION

BLACK-TIE BOYS

From left, Gary Spicer, Richard Sterban of the Oak Ridge Boys, country singer Ronnie Milsap, Ernie and onetime Tiger Darrell Evans gather for a photograph.

A SONNY FORECAST

Longtime WWJ weatherman Sonny Eliot and Ernie were among the broadcasting legends saluted during the 2008 Detroit's Classic Radio Voices exhibit at the Detroit Historical Museum.

COURTESY OF THE DETROIT HISTORICAL SOCIETY

HOLLYWOOD APPEAL

Ernie, Billy Crystal and former Detroit mayor Dennis Archer strike a pose at Tiger Stadium in 2000. Crystal filmed part of the HBO baseball movie "61*" at the stadium.

JOHN COLLIER

ON THE AIR

Ernie Harwell's most memorable broadcasts:

1
Bobby Thomson's home run in 1951 that won a pennant for the New York Giants.

2
Jim Northrup's triple in seventh game of 1968 World Series between the Tigers and Cardinals.

3
Kirk Gibson's two home runs in fifth and final game of 1984 World Series between the Tigers and Padres.

4
Bucky Dent's game-winning home run in 1978, one-game American League East playoff victory at Boston, won by Yankees.

5
Near-perfect game by Tigers pitcher Milt Wilcox at Chicago in 1983, broken up by Jerry Hairston's line-drive single to center with two outs in ninth.

BY MIKE BRUDENELL

EISENHOWER SIGHTING

Ernie with David Eisenhower in 1970. Eisenhower, the grandson of former President Dwight D. Eisenhower, threw out the first pitch that year for the Washington Senators' season opener against the Tigers in Washington.

COURTESY OF THE ERNIE HARWELL SPORTS COLLECTION, DETROIT PUBLIC LIBRARY

WILLIAM ARCHIE

COURTESY OF THE ERNIE HARWELL SPORTS COLLECTION, DETROIT PUBLIC LIBRARY

WITH THE ILITCHES

Marian Ilitch, Ernie Harwell and Tigers owner Mike Ilitch appear at a reception for the dedication of the Ernie and Lulu Harwell Room at the Detroit Public Library in 2004. The Harwells have donated so much to the library over the years that as a public collection it is second only to the National Baseball Hall of Fame in Cooperstown.

THE UECKER SEATS

Ernie and Bob Uecker share a laugh during All-Star Game festivities at Milwaukee in 2002. Uecker has been the Milwaukee Brewers' play-by-play radio broadcaster since 1971.

COURTESY OF THE KILPATRICK FAMILY

AN USHER TO REMEMBER

Shown here in 1991, Dennis Kilpatrick, left, worked as an usher for the Tigers for 44 years until his death in 2009. A part-time job became a lifelong passion. He was buried in a Tigers tie.

"I've written a few songs. Some say I've had more no-hitters than Nolan Ryan."

HARWELL, *ON HIS HOBBY OF SONGWRITING*

COURTESY OF THE ERNIE HARWELL SPORTS COLLECTION, DETROIT PUBLIC LIBRARY

KODAK MOMENT

Ernie knew Bill Eisner from his days as a photographer for the Tigers. Eisner is also known for his award-winning photos with the Detroit Fire Department.

PRIME-TIME PLAYERS

Ernie and Dick Vitale both knew Detroit well. Vitale coached the Detroit Titans and the Detroit Pistons in the 1970s before a Hall of Fame broadcasting career.

COURTESY OF THE ERNIE HARWELL SPORTS COLLECTION, DETROIT PUBLIC LIBRARY

ALL-STAR MOMENT

Ernie shares a hug at the 2005 All-Star Game at Comerica Park in Detroit. He returned to the booth to call one at-bat during the game's fourth inning. Asked about the standing ovation from the crowd as he walked on the field before the game, Ernie replied: "It made me feel great. It was a warm, fuzzy feeling."

AMY LEANG

LAST HOME OPENER

Ernie acknowledges the Comerica Park crowd during the 2002 home opener — his final Detroit opener as Tigers broadcaster. "Here in Detroit and in Cincinnati, those are the two places where Opening Day is an event," Ernie said. "In other cities, sometimes it's ho-hum, sometimes it's a big event."

JULIAN H. GONZALEZ

THE FINAL YEAR

CALLS FROM *THE VOICE OF SUMMER*

SEPT. 29, 2002: *ERNIE HARWELL'S FINAL GAME AS TIGERS BROADCASTER, A 1-0 LOSS AT TORONTO:*

"TWO DOWN, A MAN ON, MR. ESCOBAR TRYING TO GET THAT FINAL OUT. PENA DIGGING IN, WAITING. HERE'S THE SET, THE PITCH. SWING AND A MISS, AND THE TORONTO BLUE JAYS WIN THE FINAL GAME OF 2002. THE FINAL SCORE, THE BLUE JAYS ONE AND THE TIGERS NOTHING."

ERIC SEALS

LINEUP CHECK

Ernie fills out his lineup card before the start of
the 2002 exhibition opener against the
Pittsburgh Pirates. The Tigers started 0-11 that
season and finished last in the American League
Central at 55-106.

ERIC SEALS

> "When I see a statue, I think of history. Of Washington and Lincoln, generals Grant and Lee. I don't deserve a statue or part of history. But let me tell you, from my heart, I'm proud this statue is me."

HARWELL, *ON THE DEDICATION OF A STATUE IN HIS HONOR AT COMERICA PARK IN 2002*

LOVE OF THE JOB

Ernie looks over the lineup as a fan waits for him to sign a baseball. "He's the most gentle, the most tolerant, most patient man I've ever met," longtime broadcast partner Paul Carey said. "He's just one of a kind. There will never be another Ernie."

ONE MORE TURTLE SIGHTING

Ernie looks around Joker Marchant Stadium in Lakeland, Fla., before his final spring training opener as Tigers broadcaster in 2002. He would later recite his "Voice of the Turtle" verse for the last time to open a season.

ERIC SEALS

Radio silence

BY JOHN LOWE

In 2002 at Toronto, Ernie Harwell felt emotion overtake him once during his final Tigers broadcast. It happened a few moments after the game, when he read his farewell address. Holding his printed copy of the address, he pointed to the line where he almost couldn't keep going. "It was down here," he said, "where I said, 'I might have been a small part of your life, but you've been a large part of mine.'

"I felt almost teary, almost choking. I began to say to myself, 'Am I going to get through it or not?'"

He said those emotions welled in him because "I felt so much affection for the fans. I don't think it had to do with my leaving. My appreciation for what people have done for me is so deep and so true."

Despite that flood of feelings, the man who in his 55-season major league career missed two games — neither because of faulty health — kept the words coming.

In the 1-minute, 15-second farewell address, and as usual during the game, Harwell used the spare and sturdy style he learned as a newspaperman from his Atlanta Constitution sports editor, Ralph McGill, more than 60 years ago.

"Two down, a man on, Mr. Escobar trying to get that final out," he said, enthusiastically anticipating the game's climax. "Pena digging in, waiting. Here's the set, the pitch. Swing and a miss, and the Toronto Blue Jays win the final game of 2002. The final score, the Blue Jays one and the Tigers nothing."

Break to commercial. The time was 3:18 p.m.

It had been one more classic Harwell broadcast.

At 4:11, he walked out of a broadcast booth for the last time as a major league announcer.

His prodigious résumé had one noticeable blank.

He never broadcast a perfect game.

But he broadcast thousands of games perfectly.

ALL EYES ON ERNIE
Ernie is cheered by fans as he gets his first look at the Ernie Harwell statue, which was unveiled at the main Comerica entrance in 2002. It was done by Lou Cella, co-sculptor of the Tigers statues beyond the left-centerfield fence at the park.
CHIP SOMODEVILLA

SEPT. 29, 2002: *ERNIE HARWELL'S LAST ON-AIR MOMENTS AFTER HIS FINAL GAME AS TIGERS RADIO BROADCASTER ON SEPT. 29, 2002, AT TORONTO:*

"The Tigers have just finished their 2002 season. And I've just finished my baseball broadcasting career, and it's time to say good-bye. But I think good-byes are sad, and I'd much rather say hello. Hello to a new adventure.

"I'm not leaving, folks. I'll still be with you, living my life in Michigan, my home state, surrounded by family and friends.

"And rather than good-bye, please allow me to say thank you.

"THANK YOU FOR LETTING ME BE PART OF YOUR FAMILY. THANK YOU FOR TAKING ME WITH YOU TO THAT COTTAGE UP NORTH, TO THE BEACH, THE PICNIC, YOUR WORKPLACE AND YOUR BACKYARD.

"Thank you for sneaking your transistor under the pillow as you grew up loving the Tigers.

"Now I might have been a small part of your life. But you have been a very large part of mine. And it's my privilege and honor to share with you the greatest game of all.

"Now God has a new adventure for me. And I'm ready to move on. So I leave you with a deep sense of appreciation for your longtime loyalty and support.

"I thank you very much, and God bless all of you."

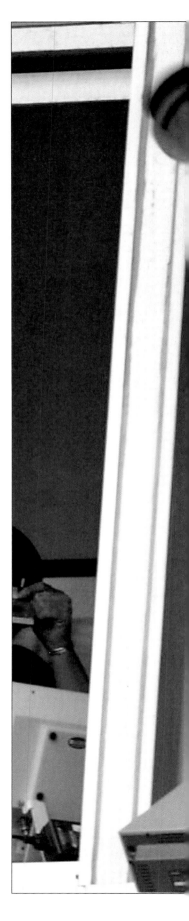

HATS OFF TO ERNIE

Ernie tosses his cap to the crowd during the seventh-inning stretch of his final home broadcast on Sept. 22, 2002. The Yankees beat the Tigers, 4-3, on that Sunday afternoon at Comerica Park.

JULIAN H. GONZALEZ

KIRTHMON F. DOZIER

A DAY TO REMEMBER

Lulu and Ernie were honored as part of Ernie Harwell Day at Comerica Park on Sept. 15, 2002. Ernie, who was retiring later that month, was showered with praise, gifts and tributes in an hour-long pregame ceremony.

KIRTHMON F. DOZIER

42 YEARS OF SERVICE

The Tigers gave Ernie a No. 42 jersey to signify the number of years he spent with the club. The number also is the only one retired throughout baseball in honor of Jackie Robinson, who was a member of the Brooklyn Dodgers in 1948 when Ernie got his major league start.

CHIP SOMODEVILLA

BRONZE BROADCASTER

Tigers great Al Kaline once said that if he had a statue, Ernie should have two at Comerica Park. He is loved that much by Tigers fans.

WAVE OF SUPPORT

Ernie salutes the Comerica crowd during Ernie Harwell Day in 2002. Longtime broadcast partner Paul Carey, Al Kaline, former Tigers president John McHale Jr. and Dale Petroskey, president of the National Baseball Hall of Fame, were among those to give tribute speeches.

KIRTHMON F. DOZIER

CHIP SOMODEVILLA

SIGN OF THE TIMES

Tigers fans Al Kowalski of Sterling Heights, left, and his nephew Scott Matties of Macomb Township show their appreciation for the legendary broadcaster during Ernie Harwell Day at Comerica Park in 2002.

FREE PRESS FILE PHOTO

RINGING THE BELL

American Stock Exchange Chairman and CEO Salvatore F. Sodano, left, applauds as Ernie reacts to a warm welcome from floor traders after he rang the opening bell at the American Stock Exchange in New York on July 17, 2002.

CHIP SOMODEVILLA

TUNNEL OF FUN

Ernie heads out of the tunnel after the pregame ceremony in his honor during Ernie Harwell Day at Comerica Park in 2002. One of the day's biggest surprises was when Ernie learned Cliff Dapper was there. Dapper was the minor league catcher traded by the Brooklyn Dodgers to the Atlanta Crackers for Ernie in 1948. It got Ernie to the majors. They had never met.

FOR THE FANS

Ernie's 5-minute speech during Ernie Harwell Day contained the charming range of personality that his listeners know so well. "Most of all, I want to thank you fans," he told the crowd. "I hope you'll bring your children and grandchildren and look at that statue and remember me . . . as someone who deeply appreciated the love and affection that you gave me over so many baseball seasons."

CHIP SOMODEVILLA

COURTESY OF THE DAN DICKERSON COLLECTION

7TH -INNING STRETCH

GEORGIA'S FINEST

Ernie, second from right, interviews Atlanta Crackers manager Paul Richards, right, for WSB in 1941. Team members pictured include Allyn Stout, Charlie Glock and Emil Mailho. Ernie got his radio start with WSB in 1940 and later did play-by-play for his home-state Crackers.

MIKE THOMPSON

MOTOWN'S GREATEST HITS

Ernie Harwell's top 10 Tigers he saw play during his broadcasting days:

1

AL KALINE

"The consummate pro for 22 seasons. A brilliant fielder and clutch hitter. Too bad this great team player appeared in only one World Series."

2

ALAN TRAMMELL AND LOU WHITAKER

"They make the list as one. Baseball's most enduring keystone combination. For almost 20 years together, they were the heart and soul of their teams."

3

BILL FREEHAN

"He caught more games than any other Tiger. A steady force behind the plate and a top-notch leader. Always there with big clutch hits."

4

LANCE PARRISH

"Freehan's equal in his own generation. He always put his team first."

MIKE THOMPSON

5
MARK FIDRYCH

"The most charismatic of all the Tigers. The Bird was always good for another 20,000 at the game — home or away. It was a shame injuries shortened his colorful career."

6
CECIL FIELDER

"The big guy was underrated. He was the most powerful Tiger of our era. Until Mark McGwire, I never had seen anybody hit a ball harder."

7
DENNY MCLAIN

"His 31-victory season in 1968 ranks No. 1 for a single-season performance. Despite his shortcomings and off-the-field problems, McLain was a proven winner."

8
MICKEY LOLICH

"Probably the most underrated Tigers pitcher. A true workhorse, he was effective as a starter and reliever. He never missed a turn and could always give you 200 to 300 innings a season."

9
JACK MORRIS

"My top gamer. He proved his worth as a winning pitcher under playoff and World Series pressure. The competitive juices flowed freely in the tightly wound Mr. Morris."

10
WILLIE HERNANDEZ

"The classic reliever. In 1984 he won the Cy Young and MVP awards after saving 32 games in 33 opportunities for the World Series champions. No Detroit bullpen star was any better for one season than Hernandez."

Behind

BY JOHN LOWE

What fellow radio voices of the game had to say about Ernie Harwell:

BILL KING
OAKLAND A'S

"When you hear Ernie Harwell's honey tones, and that wonderful timbre of the voice and the cadence, if it's in the background and you don't even hear the distinct words and phrases, it says to you, 'That's baseball.' "

JOE CASTIGLIONE
BOSTON RED SOX

"There's never been a better guy at helping young broadcasters. He knows everybody's name. He remembers them. Ernie set an example about helping these young broadcasters. I've seen him over the years with so many of them."

PAUL OLDEN
TAMPA BAY RAYS

"When I first made it to the major leagues in 1988 with Cleveland, I packed up and went to spring training. I walked into the public-relations office to introduce myself, and they said, 'Oh, here's a letter for you.' I thought, 'Who knows I am here?' I opened it, and it was a welcome-to-the-major-leagues note from Ernie. He had no idea who I was, but obviously he wanted to welcome me to the big leagues a new kid in the fraternity."

TOM CHEEK
TORONTO BLUE JAYS

"In our first spring training, he lived near our training camp in Dunedin, Fla. He said, 'Lulu and I would like for you and your wife to come over and have a dish of ice cream.' How often are you invited in these days and times for a dish of ice cream? That's exactly what it was, and that is Ernie Harwell. There's only one Ernie."

VIN SCULLY
LOS ANGELES DODGERS

"Baseball is so much richer for having you all these years and poorer for losing you. … He's such a lovely man. He loves baseball, and he treats it with great respect and dignity."

HERB CARNEAL
MINNESOTA TWINS

"I learned about pacing on the radio from him. You don't have to talk every second. Absorb some of the crowd. Tell a little off-beat story that perhaps people haven't heard. And throw in some humor once in a while. It's kind of an entertainment thing."

JERRY HOWARTH
TORONTO BLUE JAYS

"He's bigger than the game because he lets the game take place and then he just calls what happens. I'm so impressed with how fundamental he is in his life and his calling of a ballgame. I saw things like discipline and routine in Ernie, and I said, 'I want to do that for myself.' "

RYAN LEFEBVRE
KANSAS CITY ROYALS

"Any broadcaster tells you a highlight when their team plays the Tigers is to see Ernie and talk to Ernie. I think everybody feels like he is Ernie's best friend. Then you realize you're not. Ernie just has a lot of best friends."

DENNY MATTHEWS
KANSAS CITY ROYALS

"When I was growing up in central Illinois, I had the pleasure of picking up lot of radio stations and a lot of different broadcasts and broadcasters, and I had the pleasure of listening to Ernie many a night. … Then I had the immense pleasure of working with Ernie on the 1982 American League Championship Series on CBS Radio. Just a chance to work with him, having listened to him and having known him, was unbelievable."

the mike

COURTESY OF THE DAN DICKERSON COLLECTION

THEN AND NOW

Ernie spent 37 years as the radio voice of the Tigers, and he was joined in the booth by Dan Dickerson his final three years (2000-02). Dickerson has been the team's play-by-play voice since Ernie retired after the 2002 season.

ERIC NADEL
TEXAS RANGERS

"I remember as a first-year professional radio announcer, noticing how descriptive he was, how well he used the language. A lot of people take shortcuts in radio, especially with the great spread of TV. And anytime I listen to Ernie, I'm reminded, 'Don't take any shortcuts.' You are the eyes of the audience, and nobody has ever done that as well as he does."

ED FARMER
CHICAGO WHITE SOX

"When I first started broadcasting, Ernie said, 'Edward, be yourself. Just be yourself. That's all I'm going to tell you. People will like your voice, because you have a nice, pleasant tone. Tell them where the ball is. They just want to know where the ball is. Tell them that and give them the score, and just be yourself.' True words."

DAVE NIEHAUS
SEATTLE MARINERS

"When an announcer has the longevity with a club that Ernie does, he becomes identified even more with the club than the stars. The Kalines and the icons of the game pass through here. They have exciting years like 1968, and they turn the town on. They turn the town on with their talent, and the baseball announcer turns the town on as much as he can every year with his talent, whether you win a championship or not. People tune in to listen because it's Ernie Harwell and it's baseball."

TOM HAMILTON
CLEVELAND INDIANS

"You talk about Hank Aaron, Willie Mays and Bob Gibson. You're also talking in the same vein about Ernie Harwell, Jack Buck, Harry Caray and Vin Scully. The likes of those people we'll never have again."

RICK RIZZS
SEATTLE MARINERS

"It was so important that Ernie decide when he leaves. That's the way it should have been in the first place. Then there wouldn't have been so much acrimony, like there was back in 1992 when I got here. But this is Ernie's decision. It's a good one. He's been so great to baseball, not only baseball in Detroit but around the country. He's going to be missed not only by the fans here, but folks like ourselves who get to spend time with him. He's a treasure."

JIM PRICE
TIGERS

"He's the best broadcaster I've ever heard because he keeps it simple. He and I think statistics are overused. The most important statistic according to Ernie is runs scored."

DAN DICKERSON
TIGERS

"We were in Baltimore, and my brother was there with his son. Ernie was throwing out the first pitch that day. My nephew, who is 10, watches Ernie do that and thinks that's kind of neat. All my nephew wants that day is to get a ball. My brother and I are talking in the hallway outside the booth when Ernie comes up from the field after throwing out the first pitch. He sees me with my brother, whom he's met, and with my nephew. He reaches into his pocket, pulls out the ball that he's just thrown out for the first pitch in his last game in Baltimore and gives it to my nephew, who's absolutely speechless."

ERNIE AND FAMILY

APRIL 7, 1984: *JACK MORRIS THROWS A NO-HITTER AT CHICAGO:*

"ONE BALL, TWO STRIKES, MORRIS AHEAD OF THE HITTER. STEGMAN BACK TO FIRST BASE. BERGMAN PLAYING VERY WIDE OF THE BAG ON HIM. A TUG OF THE CAP BY MORRIS. WORKING OFF THE SET POSITION NOW. HE GOES TO HIS SET, KITTLE WAITS. HERE IT COMES — HE STRUCK HIM OUT AND MORRIS HAS A NO-HITTER! LANCE PARRISH GOES OUT AND GRABS HIM, AND THE TIGERS GET A NO-HIT PERFORMANCE FOR THE FIRST TIME SINCE 1958, WHEN JIM BUNNING DID IT! JACK MORRIS, THE NO-HIT HERO, SURROUNDED BY HIS TEAMMATES. IN THE NINTH INNING, CHICAGO: NO RUNS, NO HITS, NO ERRORS, ONE MAN LEFT. AND THE FINAL SCORE, DETROIT FOUR, CHICAGO NOTHING."

WITH THE BOYS

Ernie and Lulu pose for a photo with their two oldest children, sons Gray and Bill. Gray bought Ernie his first beret while the family was staying in Spain during the winter before the 1965 baseball season.

COURTESY OF THE ERNIE HARWELL SPORTS COLLECTION, DETROIT PUBLIC LIBRARY

COURTESY OF THE ERNIE HARWELL SPORTS COLLECTION, DETROIT PUBLIC LIBRARY

THE HARWELL GIRLS

Lulu Harwell is pictured with twin daughters Julie, left, and Carolyn. The twins were born in 1958 while Ernie was a broadcaster for the Baltimore Orioles.

"Baseball is a lot like life. It's a day-to-day existence, full of ups and downs. You make the most of your opportunities in baseball as you do in life."

HARWELL, *ON HIS PHILOSOPHY OF LIFE*

TALKIN' BASEBALL

Above: Tigers second baseman Frank Bolling chats with Bill Harwell, second from left, as Gray, Lulu and Ernie Harwell look on. Bolling spent the first six seasons (1954, 1956-60) of his 12-year career with Detroit.

COURTESY OF THE ERNIE HARWELL SPORTS COLLECTION, DETROIT PUBLIC LIBRARY

COURTESY OF THE ERNIE
HARWELL SPORTS COLLECTION,
DETROIT PUBLIC LIBRARY

A Lulu of a woman

FREE PRESS STAFF

Behind many good men, there's often a good woman. Behind Ernie Harwell, there's Lulu Harwell, his wife of 68 years. The same year he began broadcasting and interviewed baseball legend Connie Mack, Ernie met Lulu Tankersley. The year was 1940. In August of the next year they married.

"It's been wonderful — she's such a wonderful person," Ernie said.

The Harwells had four children, seven grandchildren and seven great-grandchildren. Staying fit and healthy eating habits helped the Harwells enjoy a long life together. For many years, they walked together.

Wherever the Harwells lived, in Michigan or in Lakeland, Fla., during January to April, they walked their neighborhoods.

Bleak weather sent them mall-walking, usually at Novi's Twelve Oaks Mall. During spring baseball season and in Michigan summers, they walked at dusk, avoiding the day's heat.

Lulu chatted along the walks about their family and often pointed out snake holes below and trees above. She's an accomplished gardener. Ernie was more the listener, much like he was for 15 years of walks with former Tigers manager Sparky Anderson during road trips.

HAPPY COUPLE
Ernie and Lulu, shown at far left in their early years together and here in 2009, were married for more than 68 years. "When you're on the road as much as I am, you need someone rock solid to hold the fort at home," Ernie said.
MANDI WRIGHT

Another of Ernie's favorite exercises was jumping rope. Even into his 90s, he topped 300 skips many days, along with 25 lunges, 25 deep squats and 50 sit-ups — often before breakfast.

Back home, the Harwells ate healthy and kept portions small. They ate mostly fruits and vegetables, and red meat once every week or two. Ernie rarely ate ballpark food except for an occasional Milwaukee bratwurst.

"Lulu's a great cook," he said, citing her cornmeal and almond-crusted tilapia.

Ernie's weaknesses were fried apples — burned, he says, in sugar and olive oil — as well as cheese and olives. He also loved hardtack made of cornmeal and "well-cooked, burned food."

"She's the best thing that ever happened to me," Ernie said.

PEOPLE IN THE NEIGHBORHOOD

Ernie and Lulu take a walk in their Farmington Hills neighborhood in July 2003. They often walked together in Michigan, frequently hiking parts of the 211-acre Heritage Park near their home. Lulu did most of the talking during the walks.

HUGH GRANNUM

MICHIGAN MEMORIES

The Harwells, shown here in 2009, lived at the Fox Run Village senior development in Novi since September 2003. Ernie became quite popular in his building. "He knows all the men's names. And we've got 600 people in here," Lulu said in 2006.

MANDI WRIGHT

ERIC SEALS

COLLEGE SWEETHEARTS

Shown here in 2002, Ernie and Lulu met at a dance in 1940 when a fraternity brother of Ernie's introduced them while attending college in Georgia. They were married the next summer.

A BASEBALL PAIRING

Shown here in 1991, the Harwells scheduled much of their lives around baseball season. While not a great fan of the game, Lulu was a devoted follower of Tigers broadcasts: "I listen to Ernie every time I can get to a radio."

JULIAN H. GONZALEZ

MEMORIES OF ERNIE

"I would say in my time in Michigan, the two biggest people I ever met were Ernie Harwell and Bo Schembechler. And believe me, you're all very fortunate in your lives in that town to have him."

SPARKY ANDERSON

"The game of baseball produces a lot of characters, but none of them, however, has the character that lives inside the heart of Ernie Harwell.... The greatest free agent the Tigers ever picked up. He's the most beloved person in Tiger history."

AL KALINE

"Ernie's been a great friend. We did little parts in the Ty Cobb movie, and he's always been real nice to my extended family that's up this way. He's just a great voice of baseball."

ROGER CLEMENS

"Ernie Harwell's spirit has never wavered — on radio, TV, and more importantly, personally to everyone he touched. Certainly, in my case, his spirit rubbed off on me and he will always be an influence."

KIRK GIBSON

"He was so genuine in everything that he did — from his legendary broadcasting to the way he treated the fans and everyone around him. He was truly a gentleman in every sense of the word."

MIKE ILITCH

"The two people I think of when I joined the Tigers were Al Kaline and Ernie Harwell. You don't have to be just a Tigers fan to know Ernie. He's one of the best, and most respected, broadcasters in the history of the game."

DAVE DOMBROWSKI

"Ernie Harwell is beloved in this city. You will never meet a better baseball man."

JOE BUCK

"Ernie has never taken himself too seriously. He is offering entertainment as a baseball announcer. He's not here to solve world problems. He's helping people pass the time with baseball. That's part of what the magic of Ernie Harwell is. He's not hung up on himself."

FRANK BECKMANN

"I loved listening to you when I was in Cleveland. You came in loud and clear on that radio signal over Lake Erie. It was great to hear you call those games. You've had a wonderful career, and we'll miss you."

GEORGE STEINBRENNER

"He's just so kind and human and gentlemanly — my kind of people. We went to the same church together in Baltimore, and our wives were great friends. And I knew that by recommending him, nobody would ever be embarrassed."

GEORGE KELL, WHO RECOMMENDED THE TIGERS HIRE HARWELL

"I've never had a harsh word between us. I don't think anybody ever has arguments with Ernie Harwell. I have a little temper. People might get mad at me. But I don't think anybody could ever get mad at Ernie Harwell."

PAUL CAREY

TURNS IN HIS LIFE

Ernie Harwell wrote in his 1985 autobiography "Tuned to Baseball" about three miracles in life that have touched him:

1944

Three days before being shipped to the Pacific with his Marine battalion, he was told he would be needed at Camp LeJeune instead, putting out the camp newspaper. Eighty percent of the battalion was killed in battle.

1956

A waiter in a Chinese restaurant in Baltimore — without recognizing any of the men at the table — presented them with a sheet of paper and the plea: "Hey, you guys. I've got a petition here you've got to sign. We can't lose Ernie Harwell. We've got to keep him here." The diners were Harwell, his agent and a representative of the ad agency that was playing a big role in the impending firing by the Orioles after acquiring a new sponsor. The ad rep returned to New York and recommended that Harwell be retained.

1979

When one of Harwell's sons urgently needed $10,000, Ernie told him he did not have that kind of money. But within days Harwell received a telephone call from Bill James, who was manager of WJR at the time, telling him he would be given a $10,000 raise and he could "get it when you come home at the end of the week."

MR. NICE GUY

Ernie was known as one of the friendliest people anyone would ever meet. Lulu knows why: "It's Ernie's nature not to say bad things about people. His mother told me that when he was a little boy, Ernie wouldn't stand for his brothers saying anything bad about anybody."

KIRTHMON F. DOZIER

RAISE YOUR ARMS

Ernie acknowledges the
Comerica Park crowd during a
game against the Royals on
Sept. 16, 2009. He gave a
farewell address to thank fans
and the Tigers organization.
ROMAIN BLANQUART

ONE LAST CALL

OCT. 3, 1990: *CECIL FIELDER HITS HIS 50TH HOMER ON THE FINAL DAY AT YANKEE STADIUM*

"HERE'S THE STRETCH BY ADKINS, THE SET, THE PITCH. THERE'S A LONG FLY BALL TO LEFT DOWN THE LINE! IF IT STAYS FAIR, IT'S GONE! IT'S A FAIR BALL — HITS THE FACING OF THE UPPER DECK! HOME RUN NO. 50 FOR CECIL FIELDER! HE BECOMES THE 11TH MAN IN MAJOR LEAGUE HISTORY TO COLLECT 50 HOME RUNS IN A SEASON, THE FIRST IN 29 YEARS IN THE AMERICAN LEAGUE TO HIT FIVE-OH. PHILLIPS SCORES AHEAD OF HIM. CECIL HAS HIT NO. 50. IT'S SIX-NOTHING TIGERS. A TREMENDOUS BELT DOWN THE LEFTFIELD LINE. YOU HAD TO HOLD YOUR BREATH. IT TIPPED THE FACING OF THE UPPER DECK. THE CALL BY UMPIRE DAN MORRISON, WITH THE SIGNAL — FAIR BALL. AND IT'S A HOME RUN FOR CECIL FIELDER — NO. 50. NOW CECIL'S HAPPY. HE'S WAVING HIS HANDS TO THE CROWD, AND GETS SOME HUGS AND EMBRACES FROM HIS TEAMMATES IN THE TIGER DUGOUT. THEY'RE ALL HAPPY FOR HIM."

A BIG ENTRANCE

Ernie greets fans as he walks out of the tunnel to give his farewell address at Comerica. He gave his speech in the middle of the third inning.

KIRTHMON F. DOZIER

IN THE STANDS ...

Fans show their support for Ernie during his speech at Comerica Park on Sept. 16, 2009. Other signs in the stands included "Ernie Harwell is baseball," "Ernie, You're My Tiger" and "Bless You, Ernie."

KIRTHMON F. DOZIER

ON THE SCOREBOARD ...

Ernie gets a big-screen thank-you on the Comerica Park scoreboard. A video tribute showed a young, dark-haired Ernie and great moments and friends from the past.

IN THEIR EYES

Barb Hickey of Detroit, a longtime friend of Ernie and Lulu, wipes a tear from her eye as Ernie gives his farewell speech. Ernie made many friends since arriving in Detroit in 1960.

DIANE WEISS

MANDI WRIGHT

 Ernie

Signing off for good

BY DREW SHARP

Ernie Harwell is a member of the family. He symbolizes home. He's Detroit's communal uncle, a source of comfort and optimism through the vibrant images he conveyed through radio transistors. It didn't matter if you were driving several hundred miles away. When nightfall came and the radio signals bounced just right, you could still clearly catch him sitting in amazement at Mark Fidrych's 1976 rookie season or the Tigers racing to their 35-5 start in 1984.

And, suddenly, you're transported back to your back porch with your brother on a summer's evening when your only concern as an 8-year-old was whether Al Kaline could recover from his broken arm in time to play in his first World Series in 1968.

Ernie was the calm within the caldron those four searing nights in July 1967, when the Tigers were forced from town as the city burned during the riots. Police wanted home lights off, but radios were on and there was a necessary connection to some sense of normalcy.

It's always hard saying good-bye to a loved one, but celebration eclipsed sorrow for a night at Comerica Park as the terminally ill Harwell thanked the Tigers and Detroit for a life well lived with absolutely no regrets. But the roles quickly reversed, and Ernie found himself the deserving recipient of a city's love and appreciation for his simple kindness

DIANE WEISS

VIEW TO REMEMBER
Roger Farver of Midland captures the moment with his camera as his son Travis looks on during Ernie's dedication to the fans at Comerica.

and genuine humanity.

He never bailed on Detroit and was always one of its stronger advocates. Such devoted friends are scarce now. That's why it's impossible for those my age and older who've always called Detroit home to fully repay Ernie for all the joy he provided us through the decades.

A heartfelt "Thank You" was a good start.

Ernie's too modest to understand the impact he has had on so many people simply through the sheer sincerity of his spirit. They don't erect statues for that, but it's nonetheless the greatest legacy any of us can leave.

Ernie has courageously accepted the consequences of his cancer. He happily embraces whatever time remains, determined to cherish every moment. He refused to turn a tribute into a somber affair.

ONE LAST TIME AT THE MIKE

It was a night to remember in Detroit. After approval from Major League Baseball and the visiting Kansas City Royals, the game was stopped in the middle of the third inning for Ernie to speak.

KIRTHMON F. DOZIER

ONE LAST MOMENT AT THE PARK WITH THE VOICE OF SUMMER

BY MICHAEL ROSENBERG

Ernie Harwell wants us to believe he is the luckiest man on the face of the Earth. We know better. Ernie is unlucky — in his whole life, he never got to sit on his porch and listen to a live Ernie Harwell broadcast.

He has lived so long, and has been part of the fabric of Michigan for so many years, that it was easy to think he'll always be here. Harwell was the voice of summer days and nights for generations of Michiganders.

Detroit has seen Hall of Fame athletes in every sport and colorful superstars and brilliant coaches and some excellent sportscasters. But there has never been anybody like Ernie Harwell. Nobody ever performed at such a high level for so long, while staying impossibly down-to-earth. Harwell never bigtimed anybody. The mere idea of it is inconceivable.

Harwell had come to the press box to talk to his former news colleagues.

Celebrities, generally, are not as impressive in real life as you might imagine. Most Hollywood actors, even the action heroes, are short.

But when Ernie Harwell speaks to you for the first time, it is almost surreal. The Georgia accent, the perfect cadence — it's like he stepped right out of a radio. It took me a half-dozen meetings before I got used to it.

He told us he was "a failed newspaperman myself," a line that most of us in the media have heard him say often. It was always his way of bringing himself down to our level. When he was a young man, Harwell had hoped to write for the Atlanta Constitution, but fell into television and radio instead.

He said that 50 or 60 years ago, sports writers did not have to work nearly as hard as they do today. I can't imagine any of you care about that, nor should you. I mention it not for what it says about writers, but for what it says about Ernie.

He has always lived in the present. Always. He never became an old grump who talked about how great the world used to be. He loves telling stories about the past, but only because he finds them interesting.

We can only hope we handle our final days with as much grace as the classiest broadcaster anybody ever heard.

CROWD PLEASER

The standing ovation at Comerica Park took less than a minute before Ernie cut it off: "Thank you, very much. We don't want to be penalized now for the delay of the game."

KIRTHMON F. DOZIER

BY BILL MCGRAW

"We love you, Ernie," yelled the man from Flushing, as Ernie Harwell walked up the tunnel and onto the field at Comerica Park on this night.

A short, touching speech was his final stop of the night. It was delivered from the spot just above the olde English D that is painted on the grass behind home plate. And it capped an evening at the ballpark that was both jubilant and sad as Harwell, who is 91 and suffering from inoperable cancer, bid his fans farewell.

Deftly quieting the crowd's long standing ovation, Harwell jokingly said we didn't want the Tigers to be penalized for delay of game.

"Yes, we do," screamed a man from Roseville.

For 42 seasons, starting in 1960, Harwell's Dixie-tinged voice and literate, laid-back play-by-play were as much a part of Michigan summers as cherries, boat rides and humidity, and people have responded to the news of his illness — and his forthright, peaceful acceptance of his impending death — with a huge outpouring of love.

During his career, Harwell also became known as the nicest guy in Detroit, and that amiability was on display as he journeyed from the Tigers' clubhouse to the umpires' locker room to the second-deck press box to the field, accompanied by Tigers officials and his attorney and confidant, Gary Spicer.

In preparation for Harwell's pregame visit with the players, Tigers manager Jim Leyland held special team meetings to explain the immense place Harwell holds in the hearts of Detroit fans.

"A lot of these guys didn't know Ernie Harwell. And you know, Ernie Harwell is one of the biggest sports names in Michigan," Leyland said.

Harwell, who got know many of the greatest ballplayers in history, told the Tigers how much he admired their talent and said they should never listen to old-timers who say the level of talent was higher in the good old days.

The players listened reverentially, and many shook his hand when he was finished.

In the third inning, Harwell walked slowly under the stands, accompanied by his small entourage. He sat quietly in a chair, waiting for the inning to end, then walked out of the tunnel into the cool night air. He thrust his fists into the air. The crowd roared, the lights shined brightly.

After his speech, Harwell walked up 18 steep steps to the first-floor concourse. Making his way to the stadium garage, he greeted Comerica employees and thanked Tigers president Dave Dombrowski.

"Dave, you don't know how much I appreciate what you guys did for me tonight, " Harwell said.

Then, Harwell said good-bye to the people who had traveled with him on his final journey to the ballpark.

"Godspeed, everybody," Harwell said.

CALLS FROM THE VOICE OF SUMMER

"Thank you very much. We don't want to be penalized now for the delay of the game, but I do want to express my feelings here. It's a wonderful night for me. I really feel lucky to be here, and I want to thank you for that warm welcome.

"I want to express my deep appreciation to Mike Ilitch, Dave Dombrowski and the Tigers for that video salute and also for the many great things they've done for me and my family throughout my career here with the Tigers.

"IN MY ALMOST 92 YEARS ON THIS EARTH, THE GOOD LORD HAS BLESSED ME WITH A GREAT JOURNEY. AND THE BLESSED PART OF THAT JOURNEY IS THAT IT'S GOING TO END HERE IN THE GREAT STATE OF MICHIGAN.

"I deeply appreciate the people of Michigan. I love their grit. I love the way they face life. I love the family values they have. And you Tiger fans are the greatest fans of all. No question about that. And I certainly want to thank you from the depth of my heart for your devotion, your support, your loyalty and your love. Thank you very much, and God bless you."

ROMAIN BLANQUART

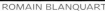

MANDI WRIGHT

"Tiger Stadium has been my home away from home. I've spent as much time here as I have in my own family room. ... Nobody's ever had a better place to work."

HARWELL, *ON HIS FINAL GAME AT TIGER STADIUM*